With God
Nothing Is Impossible

With God Nothing Is Impossible

A Canadian Life

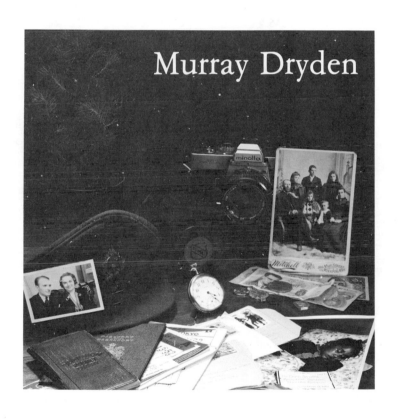

Murray Dryden

Fitzhenry & Whiteside

To Margie
who always understood me
this book is dedicated
as is every worthwhile thing
I have ever done

©1985 Fitzhenry & Whiteside
195 Allstate Parkway
Markham, Ontario L3R 4T8

Editor   Frank English
Design   Glenna Munro
Typesetting   Jay Tee Graphics Ltd.

Canadian Cataloguing in Publication Data

Dryden, Murray, 1911-
  With God nothing is impossible

ISBN 0-88902-544-4 (bound). — ISBN 0-88902-541-X (pbk.)

1. Dryden, Murray, 1911-   2. Christian biography -
Canada. I. Title.

FC27.D79A3 1984   971.06'092'4   C85-098795-4
F1034.2.D79A3 1985

Picture Credits:

Family, business, Sleeping Children Around the World,
sports and travel photographs, cards and
materials are from Murray Dryden's personal collection.

Dave Barr   top right 19,71,147,150,152, *jacket front*
Glenbow-Alberta Institute   42
Ontario Ministry of Industry and Tourism   35
Prudential Life Collection   111
Toronto Transit Commission   top 38

Contents

Foreword

In the past few years, a growing number of men and women have begun to tell us that we are losing our capacity for compassion, that we must rediscover it and – in an age when governments can no longer finance every desirable need – put it to use in the service of others.

That is a principle many of us find reasonable and agreeable. But it is one Murray Dryden lives. That is one reason why I believe that the memories recounted in these pages, so casually and so clearly, have a message of enormous importance to ourselves and our communities. For above everything else, Murray Dryden's life has been shaped and directed by a set of values that puts others first. Even the most discouraged of us knows how much we need to recover something of that set of values for ourselves and for the Canada of our grandchildren.

I first came to know Murray Dryden, in the late sixties, when he wrote me a letter (I was a columnist on *The Globe and Mail* at that time) taking courteous issue with me over a criticism I had made of the market system. He is, along with his dedication to humanitarianism, an advocate of personal initiative, conviction that comes not just from his father and mother, but from his experience of The Great Depression, in which he found struggle to be a doorway to survival.

His book has a remarkably Canadian personality. Here we have the feeling of a prairie childhood; here we meet a father who, having worked the land on one Sunday, would regret it the rest of his life; here we see a young man riding the rails of the thirties trying desperately to retain a small sense of dignity. This is a Canada we must never put behind us.

In the years in which I've known Murray Dryden I have come to sense about him an integrity that is deep – and as unbending as any I've ever known. For example, his charitable program, *Sleeping Children Around the World* – through which over 85 000 beds have been given to homeless children in third world countries – might benefit if the people who offered considerable time and services, were given income tax exemptions. But Dryden's sense of what is ethically correct says no to any such idea. A contribution of time, goods or services, must not be subsidized by taxpayers. "The people who join us, for overseas travel," he once told me, "are not only giving

6

of their time, but are sacrificing monetarily. Moreover our love of Canada and our values insist that it is more important to be morally right than legally right."

He has given enormously to untold thousands of children in the alleyways of history. But he has given to us as well. There was never a period when we stood in more need of what he offers: a life of integrity and sacrifice.

KENNETH BAGNELL
April 2, 1985

Acknowledgements

It would be impossible to list the names of all the persons who have contributed in some way to the realization of this book. While Margaret has supplied much of its inspiration. I have kept the manuscript away from her (one of my few secrets). I hope she likes it.

To Mrs. Bob (Jean) Berry, neighbour, friend, SCAW supporter and *volunteer* editor I owe a great deal. She kept me on track, diplomatically shaking off my many feeble attempts at picturesque speech that could be better described as Dryden-isms and non-words! Jean's love for Sleeping Children Around the World shines throughout the story.

Too, I want to thank Joan Seager for her contribution back in the seventies when the whole thought for this work was in its embryo stage.

I wish to express my appreciation to Nancy Garbe, long-time generous donor to SCAW for gratuitous typing services.

The things related in this book are true as I remember them. For the errors I alone am responsible.

Introduction

During the lengthy period of putting this book together, many themes came to mind. However, for various reasons, none seemed to entirely fit the manuscript.

One Saturday night – February 14, 1980 – in Quezon City, the Philippines, where we had just completed a large distribution for *Sleeping Children Around The World* (an organization founded in 1970 for the children of Developing Countries), Lieutenant Raven Salegumba asked if I planned to go to church the following morning. When I replied affirmatively, she suggested my taking a Jeepny from the Algo Inn, as it was too far to walk. However, come Sabbath morning, and with forty minutes at my disposal, I elected to walk.

It was quiet for Manila, and my mind was working overtime – something that could never happen with the noisy din of a Jeepny. I had just reached the half-way mark when, suddenly, these words burst through: "*With God Nothing is Impossible!*"

I was so excited that I seemed to become airborne. The more I thought about it, the more I knew this was it . . . . Those five words related perfectly to the manuscript theme and, in a real sense, the story of my life.

Later, at 10 a.m. at the church service, you can imagine my stunned disbelief when the Salvation Army Captain rose and said, "We will open our service by singing 'Nothing is Impossible'." I had never known there was such a hymn, but after the service I was able to procure a copy of its music and words to bring home.

Then, two weeks later, as I departed Palu in Central Celebes, following a large distribution there, a petite Chinese doctor, Dr. Suryani Angjaya, from the Salvation Army Hospital, presented a small parcel to me. Upon opening it, to my amazement I found it contained a lovely brown, black and white batik banner, which now graces a wall in my office. It reads: *With God Nothing is Impossible!*

All royalties from the sale of this book go to Sleeping Children Around the World.

MURRAY DRYDEN
Toronto
August, 1985

CHAPTER ONE

Early Family Life

In 1834, Andrew Dryden left Hawick, Scotland for Canada, taking with him his family of nine and some of his sons' wives to settle in Dumfries Township, near Galt (now Cambridge, Ontario, Canada). In 1984, the 150th Anniversary of the Dryden Clan's emigration to Canada was observed at Cambridge.

I have been told that I was born in the Winnipeg General Hospital on 14 October 1911. In a diary that Dad kept of his 1912 trip to Toronto, to attend the Laymen's Conference of the Presbyterian Church of Canada, I found a picture notation about my physical attributes: "Just look at the chest of that baby!"

My first recollection goes back to Christmas, 1917. I recall a soldier's uniform being given to me by my grandfather. It did not fit and my father's opinion was: "The War is almost over and, by the time it is sent back to the T. Eaton Company for adjustment, it will be unlikely that you will get much use out of it." I was bitterly disappointed!

Strange that my next recollection also concerned that War. My Dad's brother, Uncle Jack, had just returned and was invited to our house for dinner. Mother went all out, laying out his favourite dishes, including gooseberry preserves.

Dryden family coat of arms

The Dryden family homestead in Hawick, Scotland; the house still stands

Andrew Dryden (Murray's grandfather), wife, Maggie, and family

Andrew at 6 years, Edna (4), Murray (10), Robert (2), and Helen (8); in 1921

DRYDEN TRACT

The Dryden Tract is part of the original 900 acres purchased by Andrew Dryden, wife Janet Cairns and family in 1834, when they emigrated from Hawick, Roxburghshire, Scotland. The family were Ann (Dryden) Rae - Thomas - John - Robert - Jane (Dryden) Brown - Andrew - William - James and Walter.

ERECTED 1982

Plaque commemorating the Dryden family's first property in Canada

My next item of recall must go back to 1918 or 1919 for it concerned the influenza epidemic. Apparently everyone in the family got it except me. Mother was dragging herself around looking after my four younger brothers and sisters. The kitchen floor had not been scrubbed for dear knows how long. I offered to do it, scraping it first and then soaking a small patch at a time. There was no problem seeing where I was going, and the job took me most of the day!

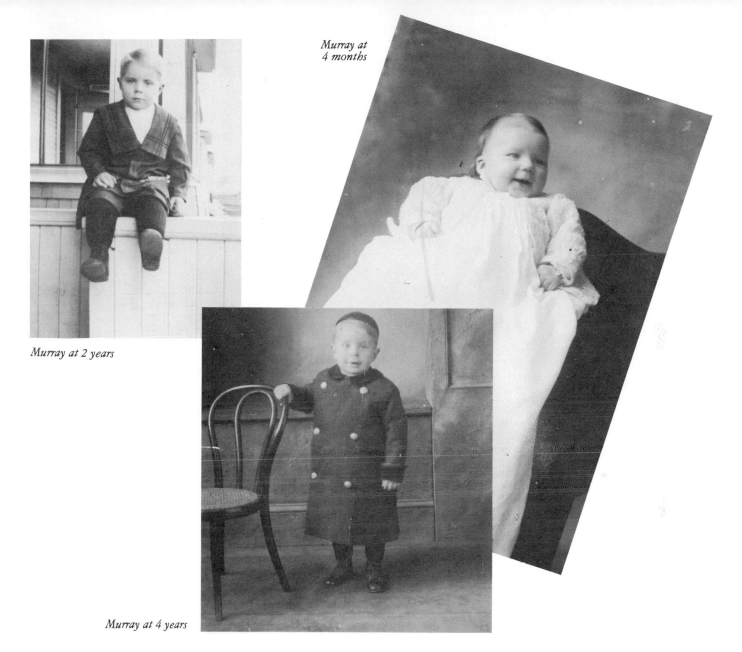

Murray at 4 months

Murray at 2 years

Murray at 4 years

Dad had bought the farm – 480 acres – in 1909 at Domain, Manitoba after homesteading at Osborne for three years. This was the year he and my mother (Amy Timlick from Arnaud, Manitoba) were married. A frame house was built and, late in 1924, a large addition was added and the whole structure given a coat of stucco. About the same period, another 240 acres were acquired to the west of us. Over the years, this property was beautifully maintained by my brother Robert and his family and now by their sons Bill and Blair Dryden. It was, and still is, a treat to travel back to the old home and reminisce about the many happy times of earlier years. Such trips have also furnished enjoyment to our children and their children.

Dryden farm in winter at Domain, Manitoba

SCHOOL DAYS

In our little community called Avonlea, we had a small Grammar School where Grades 1 to 8 were taught. Avonlea Elementary was two and a half miles from our home. We usually rode there with a horse cart in good weather and a cutter in winter.

Restricted to one acre of ground, most of our sporting activities took place in an adjoining farm field, where we played baseball in summer and "Steal the Wedge" in winter.

While far from being a brilliant student, I nevertheless achieved adequate passing marks. In that time, I received two strappings for misdemeanours. One of these was administered by Miss Esther Kemp – later the wife of Ab Gowanlock of curling fame. On that particular morning, I was doubly frightened as I faced her in the lobby "spectacle-less". It was the first and only time I had ever seen her not wearing glasses. I guess that she had not wanted anything to inhibit her stroking me with the strap four times on each hand!

During my days at public school, I developed a real feeling of inferiority because of *shoes*. Mr. Yarwood, who ran the General Store at Domain, retired, sold the business and liquidated his inventory. He had shoes that must have been purchased at the turn of the century. Unfortunately, one pair fitted me, and the price was right. I think they were the shoes that came out just before the buttoned ones. Oh man, did they squeak!

Every time I took an assignment up to the teacher, those clogs would howl, but the sound was usually drowned out along the way by snickers. I did everything – even soaked them overnight in a bucket of water. And, of course, there was no "wear-out" to them! Just when I was finally able to part company with them, my Uncle Jack offered my Dad his wedding shoes. They were too

Murray's father, Uncle Ed and Uncle Jack

14

small for Uncle Jack and he had only worn them on his wedding day. Naturally they fitted *me*, so I inherited them! They were long and black and had the sharpest pointed toes. The boys at school used to tease and say they saw the points coming around the corner before they saw me. They would not allow me to kick the football with them for fear I might puncture it. My cousin, Morley Whillans, razzed the life out of me when I visited his family during summer vacation, because of those shoes.

Possibly my most vivid recollection of early school days concerns Arbor Day. This particular year, I ate my peas and later graduated to the kernels of corn. This all brought on thirst. About a half mile from home the jig, jig, jig of the cart produced the most violent stomach ache imaginable. Finally, when I thought I was about to die, I turned over the reins to my brother. I left the cart, got down on the clay road and rolled over and over for a whole telephone-pole distance. What a relief as I brought up my vegetable garden!

The closest high school to our farm was the Convent at Ste. Agathe – seven and a half miles distant. It was there that I attended Grades 9 and 10, travelling on horseback. Classes began at 8:30 a.m., and I was late only the first morning in those two years – and then because I did not know how much time to allow. I soon discovered that I had to leave at ten minutes after seven in summer and ten minutes to seven in winter. As the horse had to have one hour to feed before starting out, this meant rising around 5:30 a.m.

It was a brisk ride in winter on the Prairies when temperatures often sank to -40° Fahrenheit. I was lucky in the morning in that I was travelling in a southeasterly direction. The sack of hay on the back of the saddle sheltered me from the onslaught of the frigid northwest wind. However, it was a different story at night as I had to face the wind, and, of course, my horse had eaten the sack of hay at noontime!

My third year of high school took me to Sanford Consolidated High School, where I boarded Monday to Friday at the home of Mr. and Mrs. Luke Parker.

I was a real dunce in Algebra and failed my final Grade 11 examination. I tried the "supp" later – only to get an even lower mark. On that note, I completed my formal academic education.

I had been fortunate, though, to be able to participate in the Manitoba Spelling Competition held at the Walker Theatre in Winnipeg in 1927 and provincial oratorical contests in 1927 and 1928, staged at Carman, Manitoba. My two speeches (still in my file) were entitled "Canada's Future" and "Canada's People".

My sisters Edna and Jean took their Grades 9 and 10 all by correspondence, converting their bedroom into a study and setting up rigid work schedules. As the student minister usually stayed with us, he would frequently tutor the girls when he was not in Winnipeg at college.

Avonlea had lots of bachelors and so our "school-marms" were always vulnerable to marriage. As soon as a school teacher was "plucked off", an advertisement would go in the *Manitoba Free Press* listing the requirements and the usual $800 salary.

Sanford Consolidated High School, where Murray studied in 1928-1929

Avonlea school kids, 1933-34

It was not unusual to have upwards of eighty applicants for the job. Around the end of July, Dad, as secretary-treasurer, would call a meeting of the Board Members and they would meet at our home. I can still see them gathered around the kitchen table with the applications placed in the middle of the table. The first thing they would do was eliminate all the poor handwriters – even if one had a PhD, it mattered not. While it seemed an unintelligent approach, we nevertheless did acquire a fine series of school teachers over the years.

My father was the perennial secretary-treasurer of the School Board. Occasionally, the teacher was also boarded at our place and paid us $20 a month for room and board.

SPECIAL DAYS

How I used to enjoy the district fairs, picnics, sports days, and other special days! My parents took us to most of the sports days and, because I was quite "fleet of foot," they rarely had to pay for refreshments, as I usually won cash awards.

The baseball tournaments were always fun, and how those farmers could heckle the players! A waning pitcher was usually subjected to the derisive observation that he had drunk either too much Green River or dandelion wine.

One year, at the first practice of our ALS (officially, the Avonlea Literary Society – but unofficially and better known as the Avonlea Lunatic Society), my Dad was playing centre field. I saw him take off like a jack rabbit after a screaming liner that he fielded, by a shoestring catch, off the nibbled grass of Charlie Harrison's pasture field. It was the third out. Dad came back to the bench and threw down his glove; I was not to see him play again. I never did find out if he was a fine player or if, when he made that spectacular catch, he decided to quit when he was ahead.

LIFE ON THE FARM

Dad belonged to the Farmers' Cooperative and purchased a lot of things, such as coal and flour, through it. Each fall, the flour order was twenty-four 100-pound

Dryden farm at Domain in summer

sacks. Mother, who was a marvellous cook and rarely followed a recipe, used almost 50 pounds of flour a week. Our farm was a mecca almost every weekend for friends and relations from the City. Mother was used to preparing lavish spreads for the urban hordes.

One weekend, a cousin of my Dad visited us for dinner and Mother turned handsprings to entertain him. When she asked if he would have tea or coffee, he replied, "Milk". Mother said apologetically, "I'm sorry, our milk has turned due to the extreme heat." He replied that cream would do. Again Mother, by this time red-faced, had to give him the same answer, to which he replied, "Poor farmers, what do you do for a living?" Afterwards Mother said to me, "I just wish I had had cream so as to make him real sick!" (meaning "turned" cream). Of course we had no ice box in those days, and our ice, stored in sawdust, was often depleted by mid-summer.

That mother of mine was so capable, so quick and so organized. She made all our clothes, mostly from old duds of more affluent relations, including wedding dresses (!), and she could upholster furniture, too. There was all that cooking she had to do for our many visitors and then, at Harvest Time, for extra "hands".

In addition to often having to milk the cows, Mother went into raising chickens in a big way. Indeed, this sideline helped greatly in pulling us through the lean years. Often the eggs were bartered at the country general store in Domain and usually fetched 6 cents a dozen. Frequently, when the local farmers had to travel to Winnipeg, they would carry a 12-dozen crate of eggs and sit on it during the journey, thereby saving us the express charges.

Mother was a very intelligent poultry breeder, usually with a flock of over 300. In order to procure the best laying strains, each fall she would arrange for a government inspector to come to cull the "non-layers". This used to amuse my Uncle Hill Rodgers, a most successful farmer in the Sanford area – one who always seemed to do things the easy way.

Uncle Hill poked fun at Mother for falling for this "culling" malarkey. He would chide her by saying, "Amy, how can these inspectors tell whether a hen is going to lay eggs this Winter? They merely cull a few so as to secure their job. Amy, I am so convinced that I am prepared to purchase the 'culls' to supply us with our Winter needs!" Well, my mother agreed to sell them and, after the inspector's annual visit, she telephoned Uncle Hill. A few days later, he arrived in his half-ton pickup. When the crates were duly loaded with the "reprieves", I remember distinctly, on one occasion, my father going into the hen house, picking up three eggs, then slipping them under the hens as they left. Shortly afterward, there was a call from my favourite uncle: "Amy, what did I tell you? Those government inspectors know nothing. Those hens you sold me actually laid three eggs on the way home!"

While we had barely sufficient water for the weekly Saturday night bath, Mother used to take an uncommonly attentive interest in our ears! Many a time, en route to church, she would call for ear inspections of the gang in the rear seat. It was not uncustomary for her, as she bore into our ears with a dampened hand-

Aunt Mabel Rodgers at 91 years

Uncle Hill Rodgers at 93 years

Grandfather Timlick, Murray's Aunt Ina and a 1926 Chevrolet

kerchief from a front-seat position, to remark, "You could grow a field of potatoes in that ear!"

She was sensitive, too, about our wearing pyjamas. Many times she made bed inspections and caught us in our "skinnies". Plainly horrified, she would chastise us and say, "What if there was a fire – what would the neighbours think?"

On one occasion, Dad – catching Mother in deep concentration – blurted out, "Amy, if you think I am going to bang some more holes in this house, you are crazy!" She was perpetually nagging Dad to fill in a window here, put a door somewhere else. . . she simply had to save steps to accomplish her daily workload and continue raising eight children.

Years later, I dropped home early one afternoon and found my wife Margaret, resting on our bed. This was unusual, and I inquired if she was ill. She replied that she had just received a letter from my mother and, after reading all the things she had done, she felt so tired thinking of it that she just had to lie down!

We never lacked for food on the farm. My grandfather Timlick was the greatest gardener and consistently won the community garden competition. His diligence, in the extreme heat of summer, worried Mother, but her pleadings fell on deaf ears. Then we thought of a ploy! There were several beehives alongside the garden. When Grandpa became too energetic, we would slip out in the morning and lift a few racks of honey from a couple of hives. This made the colony angry. Grandpa would be hoeing along and a bee would start dive-bombing him. He would drop the hoe, circle one of the evergreens while ducking his head in and out, give the bee the ha-ha and go back and pick up the hoe. Again he would be attacked. Eventually the hoe was placed in the page wire fence. When he came in, he would usually say, "A little divil of a bee kept after me until I finally had to give up."

Grandpa Timlick, who lived with us for many years, played an important part in my life, as later my wife Margaret's mother did during the thirty-three years she spent in our home. Grandpa was a stickler for perfection. Often, striding along the headland of a field I was ploughing, he could hardly wait to look up the furrow. Later, at dinner, when Dad remarked about "Murray's good ploughing job," I would hear that Grandpa had remarked, "Yes, but it could be a wee bit straighter."

Grandpa's Waltham pocket watch was also perfect, as he would set it by the arrival of the Deloraine train stopping at Domain. More than once he would announce, "It is a little *early* this morning." His watch could never be slow. He would sit by the kitchen window, timepiece in his hand, watching the setting sun and finally proclaiming, "It is gone," and would give us the time to the actual second.

In 1935, when for the first time the West won the Grey Cup (Winnipeg Blue Bombers with Fritz Hanson defeated Hamilton Tigers on a greasy field), Mother wrote, "Murray, your grandfather, almost totally confined to his bedroom, did manage to come downstairs at half-time. He was starry-eyed as he

Grandpa David Timlick at 84 years.

said, 'Amy, that was the most exciting game I ever witnessed!' " He was witnessing it on a crystal radio set!

At 84, when death finally took him, he had never experienced a toothache, had never had a cavity and, until age seventy-six, had never lost a tooth. Only then, when a trace of pyorrhea developed in one of his teeth – and when, in those days, they had no treatment – did the dentist suggest its extraction.

No story of my early life would be complete without reference to our little Spaniel, Jip. She was a great joy to the family for over twelve years, always meeting us as we came home from school. She would follow in the furrow of the gang-plough all day long. . . .

We were rascals and taught her to "chew" gum by the hour. She taught me a valuable lesson when I was about eleven years old. . . . On that particular Christmas, after we had gorged ourselves, we placed a heaping plate of goodies outside for Jip. We watched her eat a normal amount and then go over near the garage, dig a deep hole in a six-foot snowbank, cart the balance from her plate and bury it in the deep-freeze. Then, about two weeks later, when we were all down to eating hash, we saw her go over to that same bank, dig up the bones and celebrate Christmas all over again.

At one stage, we noticed that Jip was developing a beautiful glossy coat; shortly afterwards, we caught her eating a hen's egg. She had been filching eggs from the nests! I picked up the remainder of one egg, held it to her little face and scolded her. She never touched another egg.

With the marvellous vegetables from Grandpa's garden, our root cellar in the fall was bursting at the seams! Mother canned the equivalent of 1000 quarts a year — vegetables, chicken, rhubarb and whatever fruits we could afford from British Columbia. These constituted one of our treats. Another was cornflakes, but we got those only on Sunday morning. . . it was oatmeal the rest of the week.

Talking about treats: when our parents were out of sight – having gone to

Grandpa Timlick's famous Waltham watch

Three Drydens haying. Murray's father and son Dave on the wagon, and an uncle in the field. Farming methods changed little over the generations.

Winnipeg – my brother and I would invariably attempt to make some fudge. While we had no recipe to follow, we used the components – butter, milk, sugar, occasionally currants and cocoa. Our results were usually disastrous – either too hard to even chip off the pan, or else just a granulated mess! The "fudge" usually found its way into the swill pail.

The Army and Navy Store catalogue used to come in every spring from Regina. One year, Dad said, "This catalogue has been so faithful I am going to give them an order." Among the items ordered was a bunch of khaki socks. One hot day, when pitching hay up to him, he plunged his fork into the stack and cried, "Hold everything! I've lost my socks!" He took the shrunken socks out of his boots and stretched the feet to double length and the leg part to where they almost reached his knees. He declared that next year he would get his socks closer than Regina!

And then there were the Rawleigh and Watkins salesmen, and salesmen for machinery and insurance, who seemed to invade our home when least expected, often holding up mealtime. Mother referred to them as "wandering nuisances" . . . *I knew I never wanted to be a SALESMAN!*

I especially remember the neighbourliness of the folk in our community. When anyone suffered illness, a setback or some other adversity, it was a signal for everyone to pitch in and help. Memories of that feeling of security stayed with me throughout my life.

And I remember that no one ever locked a door, yet nothing was ever stolen.

Our parlour at the farm was used only for special occasions and was separated from the dining room by always-closed sliding doors. It held the piano, above which Mother and Dad's wedding picture was hung. The furniture was protected from the ravages of the "Army of Eight" but was used as prayer rails for family worship when the Minister came for dinner. The hymn-sings around the piano on Sunday evenings were very special family times.

Saturday night was bath night. The round tub was rolled out and water, to a depth of about eight inches, was baled into it. Then we started with the youngest on up the line to the oldest – the eighth, which was *me*. I got the dirty water! Water was never plentiful. For drinking, cooking and bathing, we always had to depend on collected rain water that ran off the roof of the house into the concrete cistern.

While being the eighth had its problems, life is full of compensations: I never got any hand-me-downs from brothers and sisters.

Fall was hunting time for Dad, who was an ardent hunter and usually bagged a lot of ducks, geese, and prairie chickens in his day. He bought me a 22 rifle – single shot – when I was sixteen years of age. My first shoot was in 30-below-zero weather. I fired fourteen shots, reloading each time, at a bush rabbit 25 yards away, before finally bringing it down – by fright! I ended up with frozen ears and nose, and later lost a toenail and two fingernails.

In the winter, we hauled blocks of ice out of the Red River and packed them in sawdust in a corner of our machine shed. I tell you, we made some great ice cream in our hand-cranked machine, using cracked ice from that supply!

The wedding picture of Murray's parents hung over the piano in the parlour.

One winter, we had no water for the stock. A dry fall season had depleted the water in the ponds and dugouts. We undertook to drill for water but, after two attempts at forty-two feet, all we got was salt water. We then set up a large cooker in the yard, where we melted blocks of snow and mixed this melt water with the salt water in the outside trough for the animals.

We always hoped for a flash thaw in the spring, followed by a deep and lasting freeze. Enthusiastically, I would pull out the old rusty skate blades, clamping them to my shoes or sometimes my rubber boots. Hours were spent skating the lengthy 30 acres of the ice-covered pasture field, and I can still remember dreaming of some day emulating that great speed skater, Frank Stack, from Winnipeg!

Dreams, which I contend are just another form of optimism, played an important part in my life. They pulled me out of many a dark and hopeless day. . . as did Horatio Alger books, which I devoured.

Another indelible memory lingers, that of a time just before I left the farm. It happened in October 1929, when I was hauling wheat to the elevator at Domain. On the way home I became engrossed in the front page of the *Manitoba Free Press*, reading about the wily Connie Mack defying all the predictors by choosing 35-year-old Howard Ehmke to pitch the opener (October 8) for the Athletics against the Chicago Cubs. He struck out 13, breaking a 1906 record and winning 3-1. I was reading all this from the sheltered position at the bottom of the grain box, and it was a good thing my team of horses had a homing instinct that day.

As kids, we would carry a pail of water a mile to pour down a gopher hole in summer, but skin out of fetching a pail of the same for the house. I also remember putting oatmeal in our drinking water for the hayfield. To keep our butter from melting, we used to suspend it in a well beside the house.

As children on the farm, we navigated on bare feet most of the summer. Often following a rain we would time each other as we raced over the soft, gooey Red River gumbo between our house and the Dallings'. I think that this early background has helped me relate to the thousands of barefooted children supported by our "Sleeping Children Around The World" project in Developing Countries.

Murray (5), Andrew (1), Helen (3)

THE ANIMALS AND THE BEES

Our stable of some fourteen horses meant that each year one or more had to be disposed of as they outlived their usefulness. We couldn't afford feed for such animals during the years of The Great Depression. It was always a real wrench for Dad when that certain day came soon after the fall work had been completed. It meant having to lead the designated horse out to the dense bush, some mile away, and then shoot it.

His toughest assignment came one year when the decision had to be made to end the lives of Fred and Dan, who had toiled faithfully for some fifteen years. I never saw a "tug" that this team wouldn't tackle. To flinch was not in their make-up. While Dan could possibly have contributed for one more year, Dad felt that when they had teamed together so beautifully through life it seemed only fitting that they die together.

While my father went through this ordeal without announcing it to the family, his affection for Fred and Dan clearly exposed his conscience to us for several weeks afterwards.

Grandpa bought me three pigeons – two hens and one rooster – and did they multiply! Periodically a shoot-out provided pigeon pie.

How I hated pig-killing time, for I had to sit on the pig's belly while Dad slit its throat.

Dad believed in keeping the horses thin. He used to say, "Keep them thin – then when they get sick, you can see what's the matter with them." He undoubtedly was thinking of trying to avoid veterinarian fees as much as possible.

Each spring, Dad would thin out and shorten the horses' tails. The horse hair was turned over to me. When the "Sheeny" (as we called the rag-and-bone man in those days) came around, I dickered for the best price.

It usually fell to my lot to replace the racks in the beehives. One morning, I hurriedly donned the regalia necessary, ignoring the gap between the end of the short sleeves and the gloves, also a wee hole in the head-netting. When I raised the first lid, the fighting-mad bees, who seemed to remember our thieving their honey, came at me in a cloud. Soon, one found its way through the head-netting. I dropped the racks, smoker, and all, lighting out for the barn! I'm sure I eclipsed all Olympic records as I headed through the pump-house door. It's a wonder I survived those multi-stings.

Ours was mixed farming, which meant that there were lots of chores to do, and we all contributed from an early age. We had some 12 to 14 horses, 30 pigs, and about 20 cattle, including an average of 6 that we milked. Being the eldest, one of my first duties was to bring home the cows in the evening for milking. It always seemed the grass was greener at the far end of the pasture and so I had a good distance to go.

Around this time, Dad procured a pedigreed bull. After that, Mother no longer allowed me to fetch the cows and so my Dad had to take over that chore. Shortly after that, the bull died mysteriously . . . made me wonder if my father had poisoned it, as the bull was never replaced.

One job I distinctly disliked was milking. I suspect others in the family felt the same way as they, too, jockeyed to get out of it. However, someone had to do it night and morning. One night, coming in from the stable, it was so dark our barnyard cats were running into each other. I asked Andrew, "Is that gate open?" He answered that it was, but I walked right into it, the upper bar knocking the corner off a front tooth. A couple of years later, while I was feeding mangels to the Holstein milker, she gave me a sharp uppercut with her head, sending me reeling into the manger, where I left the other corner of that tooth.

HARVEST TIME AND SURVIVAL

Harvest was always the most exciting time on a farm. It represented the culmination of a year's work and anxiety. I think a lot was taken out of farming with the advent of the combine. Oh, there was nothing to match the thrill of the big 20-40 Case tractor pulling the 32-inch separator, followed by umpteen horse-drawn bundlewagons as they moved into our yard in the darkness, prepared to commence threshing the next day.

In the earlier years, Mother packed me off to bed, but I would watch from the window as the huge, cabbed gasoline tractor, as it turned off the road into our lane, was brought to a halt while someone raised the telephone wires over the high elevator of the enormous threshing machine.

The 20-40 Case tractor

Our neighbour Alex Kemp was still threshing when I would eventually try to go to sleep. The sound of his separator, driven by an old one-lung Mogul, drove me mad as it went chug-hah-hah-hah-chug and so on. . . .

Mother was busy downstairs preparing the table for the 6 a.m. breakfasters, who usually numbered fourteen men. And man, oh man, how they could eat! Those pallid types, brought via the "Harvest Excursion" from Eastern Canada, could surely pack it away.

The outfit was cranked up by 7 a.m. sharp and ran until noon. After a one-hour lunch break, we worked through until ten minutes to eight – enough time to stable the horses and arrive at the groaning table just after 8 o'clock.

I must not forget to mention the 4 o'clock lunches that Mother would prepare and bring out to the field. Those highly paid novices, who hardly knew which end of the pitchfork to use, sure had bottomless stomachs as they lashed into the huge meat-and-tomato sandwiches. These they washed down with coffee poured from a tea kettle with the inevitable raw potato stopper in the spout. As I grew older, I graduated from washing dishes to handling my own bundlewagon.

Often we would have lengthy periods of rain, yet the kitchen crew had to prepare three square meals for the men. When we ran into spells of incessant rain, we would have to discharge the gang and later return to Winnipeg to hire a new crew.

Over the years, I still remember harvest times as fun times. Good ol' Uncle Hill would invariably telephone us at dinnertime, inquiring what success we had threshing on that particular day. Dad would usually relate a creditable performance, but Uncle Hill could always top it. My father was not the competitive type. He refused to be baited and would, as a rule, congratulate the victor. One night, Uncle Hill got Fred Baynes instead of Dad and, upon giving him a very good bushel figure for the day, Uncle Hill said, "What were you doing all day? We had to move the equipment four times and we threshed so many more bushels." Uncle Fred replied, "I can understand that. We have a 'blower' on only one end of our machine whereas you have one on both ends!"

One day, 17 August 1923, to be exact, is indelibly imprinted on my mind. On that morning, everyone was bustling around our home as Dad was preparing to drive to Winnipeg to select and bring back the first batch of harvesters – the "stookers". Mother had just given him a long list of groceries to purchase when the telephone rang. It carried the shocking message that our bank, the Home Bank, had *failed*! How I remember Mother taking back that list and crossing out everything but the absolute essentials. . . .

On Sunday mornings in the summer we had two routines. Immediately following breakfast, every member of the family grabbed a sheet, pillow case, dish towel or the like and, while Dad used the big red sewing-machine cover, we swept and drove the flies out the kitchen screen door.

Following this, we often drove around the fields to see how the crops were progressing. On 17 July 1924, I well remember how excited everyone was about the prospects for the crop of wheat. The grain was just coming into full head.

It was an intensely hot and humid day. We went to three o'clock service that day, and it became so dark that we could not read the hymn books. A terrible hail storm suddenly began smashing the west windows in the church. In a very few minutes, it was all over and the sun was shining brightly again. We drove apprehensively towards home, seeing the terrible devastation along the way – all the time hoping that, maybe, the hail swath had missed us. It was not to be. All our great expectations for the crop had been wiped out in just a few minutes. We had to turn in with mowers and cut, rake and burn the crop. I learned at an early age the great hazards and uncertainties of farming.

In 1926 we had, possibly, the best crop-potential ever – 45 bushels each of wheat and rye, 55 of barley and 80 of oats. There were over 400 acres all cut and stooked when *the rains descended.* It rained and rained and rained some more. Wild ducks moved in, devouring the grain. Often four shotgun shells would bring down six four-pound Mallards and Canvasbacks.

We retrieved some of the stooks from the water and set them up again on higher ground. Finally we had a freeze-up but, in a few days, the snows came, burying the stooks.

I stayed home from school most of that winter as we fought to save the crop. The bundle racks went on sleighs. We would drive to what looked like a stook, shovel it out, then with hay knives cut the sheaves out of the frozen ice. I was always on the lookout for signs of white weasels, bagging more than a hundred dollars' worth of skins that winter.

We would draw the sheaves into the threshing machine, making a stack on each side of the feeder. Then it usually took a couple of hours to start the gasoline tractor with the aid of ether in the priming gas. Dad often said, "Ether will put a man to sleep but sure will wake up a gasoline engine." We would thresh the two stacks and then go through the same procedure again. This went on all winter and, by spring, we had most of the crop in the bins. Granted the grain graded "tough" or "damp", but it was worth saving.

Most of the neighbours scoffed at our battle and said they would wait until spring and handle it in a civilized manner. They were to find out that, come April, the stooks were mouldy and mice had cut the hemp bands off the sheaves and ravaged the grain, resulting in an almost total write-off.

On the night of 13 January 1928, I remember being wakened at 2 a.m. by Mother. "Murray, your mother is *sick*! Your Dad is not home. Harness up a team of horses to the sleigh and go over and fetch Mrs. Dalling!" Apparently I replied, "Have a heart, Mother!" and immediately turned over and went back to sleep.

The Vision Glorious

OUR CHURCH

THE 50th ANNIVERSARY OF AVONLEA UNITED CHURCH

1899   1949

Anniversary booklet from Avonlea Church

She pulled me out of bed and, to this day, I have never forgiven my kid sister Amy for her untimely arrival into this world.

When recently writing my siblings about family news for this book, I received this note from my sister Edna:

> "The times I remember I don't think I would want to see in print – those during the War Years when Dad was all alone, with no sons or sons-in-law to help him. It rained all the time, yet he hung on to that farm so the family could have it. He had a pretty wonderful helper in Mother."

Murray's mother, father, and sister Amy, the youngest of his seven siblings

The farmer is constantly at the mercy of the weather. He is granted just so many days after the crop is matured in which to harvest it. Often the most favourable day would be the Sabbath, but never would my father consider working in the fields on that day. However, during the war (1939-1945), I remember receiving a letter in Europe from Mother in which she described Dad's agonies on the previous Sunday. . . .

It seemed that the day had dawned beautifully and, at breakfast, Dad had talked with Mother about breaking the Sabbath. The crop was ripe and waiting. He tried to justify his proposed action: his three sons were overseas, and he felt that the country needed the grain for the War effort. He had a tremendous struggle with his conscience before he finally elected to operate the combine that day. As it turned out, it was the one and only Sunday during his life that Dad worked at harvesting a crop. Long afterwards, he still expressed regrets that he had broken the Sabbath.

DAD, MOTHER AND SIBLINGS

One January day in 1956 in Winnipeg, my father announced to Mother, "That son of ours thinks he is the only one who can print. Well, I am going to print a letter to him." (Of course, I printed merely for legibility's sake as my handwriting was unreadable.)

Dad did print a letter – a beautiful eight-page letter – put it in an envelope, addressed, and stamped it. A light skiffle of snow had fallen and he told Mother he was going out to sweep off the sidewalk. A few minutes later the paper boy came rushing to the door shouting that he had discovered Dad in a snowbank.

I went out to the funeral and carried back his letter, but could not bring myself around to opening it. However, one night about a month later, I told Margie as I got into bed, "Tonight I am going to open Dad's letter." I had been wondering if he had had any premonition, but of course he had not. It was his last act on earth and one I deeply appreciated.

When my mother was on her deathbed in the hospital, her body racked by the pain of cancer, I asked my brothers and sisters gathered around her bed, "What is the most beautiful part of Mother?" All agreed that it was her hands – yes, hands that could do anything.

We also found ourselves reflecting on times when Mother and Dad were away and we would sneak up into the attic and read their old love letters. They were good reading but hardly torrid by today's standards! When they finally retired, leaving the farm to my brother, Mother was perpetually hammering away at Dad to get the attic cleared out, saying "No daughter-in-law wants to start out with all that rubbish around." Finally, one wet Monday morning, when he could not work outside, Dad was trapped. A few years later, following Dad's funeral, Mother said to me, "Why, oh why did I insist on burning those letters? I can still see your Dad plucking them out of the fire in the barnyard and reading them over the flames."

I remembered, too, the lovely Waltham watch that Mother used to wear on her dress, and which she later sent to me. One year, when broke on Mother's Day and wanting to telephone her, I pawned the watch to pay for the long-distance call. When I finally got sufficient money to retrieve it, the watch had been sold! I was terribly upset, and even moreso when Mother inquired about it a couple of times and I had to give an evasive answer. . . am sure she knew the truth, and understood too.

It would have meant so much to me and to my parents to have been able to reminisce together about the farm and those early days through these pages. I am

Family group: standing *Andrew, Frances, Edna, Jean, Murray;* seated *Robert, mother, Helen, father, Amy*

sorry, too, that Uncle Hill is not around to read this. He passed away in 1980 at age 96 – on the threshold of celebrating, with Aunt Mabel, their 70th wedding anniversary.

My sister Edna went on to a career in Nursing, while Jean joined Frances and attended Dominion Business College. Then Jean and Frances continued on to Washington, where they worked in the British Embassy from 1942 to 1946.

Helen took her high school at Sanford, and then went to Success Business College and on to work in the office of the International Harvester Company. Amy took her high school at Ste. Agathe Convent and later trained as a laboratory technician in Winnipeg.

As for my two brothers (now deceased), Andrew had difficulty academically but was a master mechanic. Being such a perfectionist, though, he rarely made money on his contracts. Priced on a carpentry basis, the customer usually got a cabinetmaker's product. Robert, the younger, attended Manitoba Agricultural College and was a thorough farmer, a hard worker – and a worrier – and died much too young with a heart attack.

On reflection, being the eldest and leaving home so early (Helen, the eldest girl was 15 and Amy only 2), I missed the fun of growing up with my seven brothers and sisters on the farm, but this has not dampened my deep feelings and memories.

MY FIRST ENTERPRISE

At sixteen, Dad gave me an acre of land directly across the road from our home. I had indicated a desire to grow mushrooms – my very first enterprise. This came after dreamy flings of potato farming and of being a taxi driver.

We had a huge pile of manure behind our horse stable and, one would have to say, it was expendable. So, in my spare time, I would fork the dung onto a manure spreader and transplant it onto my plot. This done, I ploughed it very deeply, burying the manure. I then forked the whole acre. It was a plot with great potential when I finished, if I do say so myself.

I then asked my parents if I might go to Winnipeg that fall to seek a job to make sufficient money to purchase the necessary spawn for my mushroom enterprise. When I never did earn the required money to carry out my plans, the family planted the plot in strawberries. Stories about the quality and yield seemed to me more than exaggerated!

RETURN TO THE FARM

Returning home from Saskatchewan near the end of August in 1930, I was able to help with the last few days of threshing. I promised my parents that I would stay and complete the fall work before going back to further business challenges.

I huddled with my brother Andrew, who was four years younger, and whom Uncle Hill "bugged" almost as much as he did me. We made a three-way pact: Andrew would push the six-horse tandem on the gang plough; I would run the Hart Parr tractor extra hours, and our parents promised that they would not "spill the beans" to Uncle Hill.

My Ancestors

I did not know their pedigree
Their breeding or their worth
But this I know, they gave to me
The love of common earth.

The smell of furrows brown and wet
The love of sun and rain
Their gardens, sweet with mignonette
Will live in me again.

AUTHOR UNKNOWN

Andrew got full mileage out of his horses, and the weather was good every day during September. I pushed the tractor all day and frequently well into the night. Dad would come out to the field and plead with me to shut it off and come to bed. He said I was undermining my health. I would not listen but kept ploughing by the light of the moon or a lighted straw stack.

All went well until once, late on into the night, I fell asleep on the tractor and ploughed right through the end of the field, through another farmer's field, and woke up going through a shallow ditch of a second farmer's property. I think the changing motor sound, as it struggled out of the ditch, awakened me. Here I had ploughed almost a mile beyond our headland, and there was no way I could cover up those furrows! It was bad timing – a tactical error, so to speak – and only served as extra ammunition for my parents to insist that I go to bed.

By Saturday night, however – the last day of September – we had finished the ploughing.

After dinner, we phoned up Uncle Hill and asked how his fall ploughing was going. "Very well," he told us. "Some 70 acres – about one quarter." We told him we were *finished*. "That's impossible! No farmer has completed his ploughing." I emphasized, "Our whole farm is *black*. . . ." He still refused to believe it. In fact he drove over the next day – Sunday – to see for himself.

I tell you, my brother and I were so tickled to think we had finally beaten the pants off Uncle Hill! I always did admire his competitiveness, though.

I think Mother and Dad eventually accepted the value of our whirlwind ploughing programme that year as perpetual rains set in until freeze-up, bringing all further fall work to a complete standstill.

On the Monday morning, Dad drove me to Ste. Agathe in the rain to catch the train *to Winnipeg*.

I had made my final contribution to the farm that had meant so much to me growing up. . . .

Murray's father cultivating around 1925

Leaving Home

At the age of 17, when I left home for the first time, I began a diary which I kept going for the next four or five years. Somehow, despite all the changes in my life, and all the moves, I have managed to hold on to that diary. It's a two-ring loose-leaf notebook (The Triumph – 15¢) showing a beaver on the front. Between its thick grey cardboard covers is compressed some of the anguish as I tried to stay alive during the Depression Years by selling to housewives who really couldn't afford to buy anything.

So often, during those years, I had nowhere to sleep. I would walk the streets all night, or sleep in railway station waiting rooms, or on the floor of a variety of unheated buildings. It is possibly not surprising that I developed a special appreciation of a soft, warm, clean bed that has never left me. . . .

That fateful day, in 1929, when I decided to leave home to try my luck in the big city, Dad drove me into Winnipeg, 25 miles away. It was a cold November morning, and I remember discussing my prospects with him on the way. I told him I'd do anything except selling!

I started off by cutting a number of advertisements out of the paper, then walking around the city for several hours making applications. The only place which seemed at all interested in me was the Real Silk Hosiery Mills in the McIntyre Building. They wanted me to become one of their house-to-house salesmen.

If I had thought that selling was not for me, the idea of selling ladies' silk stockings filled me with horror! However, after running into dead-ends everywhere else, I took the job "temporarily", I told myself. It was arranged that I would board with Aunt Bertie.

For an hour I walked up and down, clutching my sample case and staring with terror at the front doors. Finally, I almost tiptoed up the steps to one door and knocked. No one answered, and I wiped the sweat off my brow! When I got up the courage to go up to the next one – I well remember that address: 24 Stradbrooke – I again prayed that no one was in, but the door opened. Mrs. McCulloch greeted me warmly and asked me in. If my introduction was terrible, my sales presentation was much worse. I even forgot to take off my overcoat, with the result that I had to continually wipe beads of perspiration off my face. I did not get an order from this nice lady, because the shades she preferred were not the ones I carried. I hurriedly told her I would check with my office about that. As I

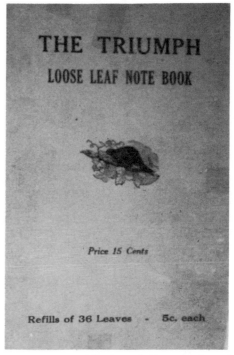

*The loose-leaf notebook used
for Murray's diary*

*The advertisement that Murray answered for
his first job*

prepared to leave, she chatted with me at the door in a kind way and I felt slightly more relaxed. In fact, Mrs. McCulloch and I remained friends for years.

Each morning, at their 8 o'clock sales meetings, Real Silk encouraged their salesmen with special "pep" songs. I guess they felt we needed them to keep us motivated in those times.

I was fortunate, that first winter, to be boarding with Aunt Bertie. She was so kind to me. I wonder to this day if she was aware that I used to head back to her house at 269 Church Avenue, about an hour before she got home, to take the edge off my appetite (with several slices of baker's bread – a treat for a boy off the farm). I had to do this in order that, at suppertime, I would not appear too ravenous and thus give away the fact that I had not been able to afford anything to eat at noontime.

Also concerned about a young man with a big appetite, who might be having difficulty satisfying that appetite on a very thin income, was – of course – Mother. When I was about to board the train at Winnipeg to go to Regina, she saw me off and slipped a $2 bill in my hand, telling me to get my lunch in the diner. She knew how I used to drool watching the diners in the dining car when the train stopped at our little village.

When I went home at Christmas, I realized that I could have called it "quits" and stayed on the farm, which my family encouraged me to do, but my pride wouldn't let me. Besides, I was determined to be able to buy sufficient spawn for my mushroom patch back home. I still had high hopes for that venture. And so, in January, I headed back to Winnipeg.

Although I was used to Manitoba winters, it seemed much worse in the city, working as I did six days a week from early morning on into the evening that first black winter of The Depression.

A vintage car at home on the farm in Manitoba

When out selling one day, I recall going into Eaton's store in Winnipeg and running into my Uncle Ed Jenkins. He gave me a terrible scolding – said I was wasting my time and that I should be home helping my Dad. This only served to make me more determined to succeed.

One night, in desperation for a place to sleep in Regina, I tried Wascana Park, but the police moved me on and I ended up spending the night walking around the streets. The next night, about midnight, I sneaked inside the Westman Chambers Building, which wasn't kept locked at night, and there I lay down on that cold terrazzo floor at the very back of the hallway on the top floor.

One of my trips out of Regina took me into Gull Lake, where I stayed at the Clarendon Hotel and the following morning went out selling.

Later, returning my sample case to the hotel room, I went down to the bus stop at the garage adjacent to the hotel and asked the first person I met when the next bus went through to Swift Current. The reply was "You are selling, aren't you? You took four orders this morning."

Then, and only then, did I notice the small brass buttons on his tunic. I had stepped up to the town's plainclothes policeman! When asked to show the orders, I took him up to my room, where he wrote down all the details – even to the colour of the stockings (gunmetal, suntan beige, etc.). Then he told me that the RCMP were on my trail and that they knew that I had done business in Shaunavon. He told me that whereas, before, first offenders were granted probation, now the minimum fine was $25, plus $3 costs. On that happy note, he left me. My total resources were less than $6. I looked out the window and there, right below, was an RCMP lorry. I was scared to death! I lay across the bed and said a little prayer. Then I jumped up and raced along the hall and down the stairs to the lady on Reception.

I asked who the town mayor was and was told it was Mr. Hutton who owned the hardware store across the street. I thanked her, rushed to the store and asked for the Mayor.

When he was pointed out at a high desk at the rear of the store, I approached him, saying, "Mr. Hutton, I'm in trouble." He answered, "I know all about it." I still proceeded to unburden my soul, to which he listened carefully and, when I had finished, he remarked, "I can see that you are young and possibly foolish, but did not intend to do wrong. I'm sure you realize that we have to protect our merchants." He then said, in an almost fatherly manner, "You leave town immediately, and I will fix it up with the Mounties." I grabbed his hand, shook it, and thanked him – then I was off.

In 1972, when Margaret and I took the western motor trip after retirement, I drove specifically to Gull Lake, hoping to find someone from the Hutton family. We spent the better part of a day looking, but came up empty. The old Clarendon Hotel was still standing – barely!

When barnstorming in the Moose Jaw, Swift Current, and Shaunavon areas on my way to Weyburn, one time, where I had planned to canvass for a week, I was given a ride by Mr. Gould, representative of Willard Chocolates. I often had a ride with him.

On that trip, I still vividly recall seeing the ditches full of soil blown off the newly seeded fields, and the crows picking up the seed. Here it is, a little over fifty years later, and the west is again plagued with soil erosion — and the new crop of farmers does not know how to cope with the problem.

It seemed strange, but everywhere I moved, some jukebox was hammering out the hit song of 1930 — "Springtime in the Rockies".

From my diary of 1930:

June 16
> Had my taste of selling in Regina. Made not one cent.

June 17
> Made three bucks after hard work.

June 18-21
> Nothing unusual. Very poor week for business. Moved Saturday night to new boarding house.

June 23-28
> Put in terrible week. Made less than $10. Slept on the office floor the last couple of nights and ate only when in dire need. Looks like a tough Dominion Day for me, but there is always a better day coming.

July 2
> Decided to join Regina Rifles (the Reserves). Spent most of the day shining buttons, etc.

July 3
> We prepared for camp. Left Armories at 11 p.m. and marched to railway station.

July 4
> Arrived in Dundurn Camp at 7:30 in rain. Had sandwich and slough coffee, and were transported to camp.

July 5
> Very warm. Hard training. Spent afternoon at Lewis machine gun practice.

July 6
> Biggest day in camp. Fought sham battle, attended church parade, and marched to Dundurn (7½ miles) at night.

July 7
> Arrived back at Regina at 7:30 a.m. Had breakfast at Kitchener Hotel; then turned in all equipment for O.K.

July 8-12
> Very poor week. No business. Still slept in office and ate one meal a day.

July 13
> Sunday. Starved. Spent day at office. Sad outlook.

July 14
> Still fasted, but finally got a break and ate.

July 20

Went to church. Wrote a number of letters; went to bed early.

July 21-26

Spent whole week recruiting men as I couldn't go outside due to carbuncle (an infection on face — due, probably, to improper food – like raw sugar by the spoonful from the landlady's sugar bowl to save on food).

Hired two men, bonded one, and ended up week with a ridiculous report. Better luck next week!

July 27 — August 2

Eventful week with the Elections (Mackenzie King defeated), the Exhibition, etc. Did not take in Exhibition for various reasons. Poor week for office with production of only $12. Made rigid preparations for next week. Ate two meals in 5 ½ days. Outlook brighter.

August 3-9

Worked like the deuce to put production over. Hired and bonded one representative for the week. Ron Graver and I decided to go to Moose Jaw. Started walking. Such an experience . . . something to talk about!

Worked hard but only made enough to take us back to Regina by train, arriving 11:40 p.m.

Somehow, I managed to last until Harvest Time, when I was hired by a farmer from Lang, Saskatchewan, through the Employment Bureau to help with his wheat crop. Several of us were quartered in a caboose with straw mattresses which, to me, felt like eiderdown after what I'd been sleeping on. We were fed four bountiful meals a day, and I ate like a vulture. In no time, I had gained twelve pounds. When Mr. Middleton saw how I handled a team of broken-down old plugs to draw my bundlewagon, he gave me a team of spirited greys which the other men were unable to handle.

Two weeks later, I was called home because Grandpa Timlick was seriously ill. Fortunately, he did get better, but I stayed on at home, wanting to make sure all the ploughing was done before I returned to the city. Mother and Dad tried to persuade me to stay with them over the winter, but I set out again in October, for Winnipeg, where I found conditions were even worse than before.

Later that fall of 1930, I wrote in my small pocket diary:

Started in again on Monday with Real Silk. Did not do much this week – about $9. Making rigid plans. Promised not to go back to Real Silk when I left, but couldn't see anything else and I simply must sell, as that is all I know.

Terrible day for business. Barth gave me permission to go out to Dauphin with Reg Carter in the morning. Stopped to sell in Portage. Vast number of experiences. . . .

Murray at Portage La Prairie, carrying his Real Silk hosiery sample case and wearing his durable Elysian wool coat, 1930

Spent evenings at the home of people called Bateman, going over every night around ten and returning to King's Hotel around 3 a.m. Wonderful rummy, '500' tournaments – and EATS! Worked hard and made about $5-$6 a day.

While we had a contract with local establishments stating that we were working for them (as a cover for lack of provincial and town licences), we were not too sure of the legality of our position. Consequently, we did "cloak and dagger" selling, never going near the main street.

On our final day in Dauphin, we had to tidy up a few items before leaving to go back to Winnipeg. I had sold a stocking order the previous day to a client who did not have the deposit ready and asked me to return for it the next morning. To conveniently reach her, I had to cross the main street. Just as I was about to sail across, I heard a gruff voice from behind say, "Heh – Wait a minute there!" Turning around, I observed a burly policeman standing in the shelter of the Safeway Store. He inquired as to what I had in my bag, and then asked if I had the necessary licences. When I told him we were working for Mr. Melnyk, the local cleaner and presser down the street, he inquired if the contract was a legal document.

I replied, "You go down and see Mr. Melnyk. He will produce the contract and I am sure you will find it OK". In my heart, I was not so sure. When he left to check its authenticity, I ran pell-mell all over town in an attempt to find Reg, finally discovering him coming out of a house. When he saw me running, he shouted, "Don't take time to tell me – just get into the car!" We drove the ninety miles to Neepawa without stopping and did considerable probing in that town until, driving past the local theatre, we noted that the movie was entitled *In Evidence*. That settled it. We continued on to Gladstone.

Here my diary says:

> Had a telephone conversation with Dorothy Murta, and arrived home in Winnipeg at 6 p.m. Worked very hard all week. . . rather discouraged as there are so many bills I would like to settle up.

Back in Winnipeg, I met Mother at Eaton's checking office that Friday. I was very glad to see her and hear all the news. Later, Mother was to say that, as she watched me disappear in the crowd, something told her I was going for a long time. (How right she was, as it was exactly three years later that I had an opportunity of a return ride west with cousin Bill Taylor. . . .)

Wanting to surprise my parents, and learning that there was going to be a fowl supper in Union Point Church that night, which I was almost sure my parents would attend, I "holed up" in the outside porch. Someone tipped me off that Mother and Dad had driven up. As Mother entered, I jumped out of the dark and hugged her. It was a complete surprise – and a terribly thoughtless thing for me to do. (She could easily have had a heart attack from the shock. Many times afterwards she would plead with me never to do that again.)

On 8 November 1930, my diary reads:

Port Arthur, Ontario   Terrible week – just made $21.05. Worked early and late, but no production. Room at Evoy's and ate out. Went to St. Paul's Church Sunday night. Left on midnight train, arriving 2 a.m. and stayed at Nipigon Inn. Had heck of an experience with Finns (95% here are Finns). Just took one order. Left on 2 a.m. train for Schreiber, using my last dime for fare.

It was important to have a productive day in order to buy my train ticket to White River. I stayed in the railway station until daylight, and then set out early to sell, picking my way through the sleepy village.

I noticed a light on in the local Roman Catholic priest's house, so I went up and knocked. The friendly Father Garçon greeted me and asked if I had any black silk socks. I did and took an order for one dozen at $13.50 with a commission of $2.

My diary goes on:

This was the start I needed for a great day — later meeting a lovely Irish girl, Kathleen O'Brien (with whom I corresponded for years). She introduced me to her aunt, a Mrs. Kelly, twisting out an order for me. Then she took me over to her bank and hammered Mr. McMullen, the young teller, into a sock order. I ended the day with $10 and sufficient to buy my fare on the 4 a.m. train, which arrived in White River at 8 a.m.

Chapleau, Ontario

I worked like the deuce in the morning and made $3.75. I left at 1:50 p.m. for Chapleau, arriving at 6 p.m. I had an interesting time getting a room.

In the CPR station I parked my sample case behind some heavy furniture, returning for it after finding the cheapest hotel. The only clothes I possessed at this stage were on my back. A vivid recollection I still have of that station, is of the brass cuspidors. One could barely see the brass as the cockroaches plied their way in and out of the spittoons!

In the morning, I called on Mrs. Sewell, the CPR superintendent's wife. She ushered me into the luxurious living room, while expressing a desire to look at my samples of men's socks. We were sitting side by side on the sofa. I pulled out the sock folder from my case and undid the fasteners. With that, at least a dozen cockroaches became activated! My prospect shrieked and rushed away for weapons. We pulled out the sofa cushions, whacking the beasts and subduing those we could catch up with. How I wished the floor would open up and swallow me! Believe it or not, I came away with an order. . . .

Continuing to work my way east, while selling to pay my fare between railway points, I wrote in my diary:

> Nothing daunted me. Slugged away all day and, at train time, had $6.10 – just enough to take me to Sudbury on 6 p.m. train. Walked streets all night – oh, what a night – storm and sleet – played right out.

Arriving with 15¢ in my pocket, I hid my case behind a hedge to save carrying it, then went into a restaurant every three hours for a cup of coffee, liberally laced with sugar, dallying as long as I could without becoming a vagrant.

After working for a day, but unable to make a thing, I started out walking at 2 p.m. towards North Bay. An inexperienced hitch-hiker, I never thumbed but just kept on walking and praying for a ride. After walking about nine miles, a driver pulled over and gave me a lift.

From my diary again:
> It was such a twisty, up-and-down road that my empty stomach commenced to do tricks, and I was frightened that I might mess up my Good Samaritan's car. We arrived in North Bay at 6 o'clock. I asked to be let out on the highway, as I was certain I could never sell anything on a Saturday night in a city.

I was still hoping that I might get *through to Toronto*. I trudged along towards Callander, ten miles distant, but no one would stop to pick me up. It was a lonely, desolate stretch of road in 1930; and I still remember the huge trees hung over the road – so unlike the prairies I was accustomed to. It was pitch dark, too, and so cold and windy. I found myself thinking of home, and almost spontaneously the words came to me: "Lead kindly light, lead thou me on. The night is dark and I am far from home. Lead thou me on." And then my eyes filled with tears. . . .

At this point, I decided to use reckless measures, almost throwing myself in front of an approaching car. When one stopped, I apologized to the driver and told him of my desperation. He said that he was only going as far as Callander but to get in. He let me out at the outskirts of what was later to become "Quintuplet Town" (because of the 1934 birth of the world-famous Dionne Quints). There were few lights. It was snowing hard and there was next to no traffic, thus making the chance of a ride most unlikely.

I had to make a decision. I remembered having passed a farm a few minutes before and I wondered if, maybe, they would allow me to sleep in their haymow. Retracing my steps, and coming upon that barn, I began dreaming of how beautiful it would be to sleep in that loft. . . .

When I knocked on the house door, a pretty girl answered; immediately all my courage drained out of me. I stuttered, sputtered, and apologized for knocking in error.

I proceeded back into the village, passing a small frame house at some little distance from the road – but not so far that I could not determine two elderly ladies knitting by lamplight. I thought maybe, just maybe, they might have a couch that I could curl up on. On knocking, one of the ladies answered and, before I could open my mouth, she invited me in. I sneaked the case in behind the door, as I did not want them to think I was peddling at this time of night. However, they were perceptive and inquired what I was selling. When I told them, they asked if I had any silk and wool hose. Before many minutes had elapsed, I had an order for 4 pair at $5.50 with a 75¢ deposit (commission).

When leaving their home, a whole new feeling came over me. I was completely buoyed up. Gone was my hunger and exhaustion. I went across the street and knocked on another house door; again I was enthusiastically invited in. Two school teachers there ordered a bunch of silk stockings, and I made another $1.75! By this time, I was almost drunk with success, and decided to tackle another house. When I knocked, I noticed through a window that a card game was in progress, so I began withdrawing to the street. However, the door opened and a lady bade me to come in. Less than a half hour later, I had another 4-pair order and 75¢ tucked in my pocket!

At this juncture, I inquired of my customer what the hotel accommodation was in town. (Just three hours earlier I had considered a hayloft!) She said that the Callander Hotel was the only place and they charged $1.50 per night. While I hated to cough up that kind of money, I was so doggone dirty and tired – remember, I had slept in a bed in Nipigon on Monday night and then not until Thursday night in Chapleau – that I felt desperate. Then the friendly lady made me an offer. She would provide bed and breakfast for $1.50 and be happy to take me as far as Powassan in the morning on her way to Mass.

After a shave and a bath and as I lay in that comfortable clean bed, I spent considerable time in reflection. How was I ever able to sell three orders of merchandise totalling over $30 in a "one-eyed" village on a late Saturday night – particularly when I was so filthy and repulsive in appearance?

The next morning, on reaching Powassan, I felt my luck running high. I got

Bay Street south of Toronto City Hall, around 1930

Murray's friend and colleague, Alex Hilson

a ride into Barrie with a police inspector, walked three or four miles more, and then was given a lift right into downtown Toronto. It was the last week of November.

Walking up Yonge Street, near College Street, I passed the Yonge Street Mission and heard hymn singing. I decided to go in. It was a great service, and afterwards they served coffee and sandwiches. This was my introduction to Toronto, and it has been one of my favourite cities ever since.

Alex Hilson and I had worked together out west for Real Silk. Alex was from Hamilton and, on 1 December 1930, he got in touch with me to tell me he had left Real Silk and was working for himself. He wanted me to help promote, in the London area, his soap and shampoo, which he manufactured and bottled in a small factory in Hamilton. This would be my entry into the cosmetics business.

Again from the 1930 Triumph diary:
London
December 8
    Made 21 calls – 21 taken back
December 9
    Read a lot in regard to Sales Distribution & Corporation at Public Library
December 10
    Spent day reviewing the different sales resistances in an endeavour to work a method of overcoming same
December 21
    St. Andrew's United Christmas service. Wonderful choir and beautiful singing

December 22
    Real nice letter from Dad
December 23
    Received a wire from Alex stating he was broke and could not come
    down. So my Xmas, I guess, will have to be spent by my lonesome self.
December 24
    Christmas Eve! And how little it seems like it. Sold shampoo in after-
    noon, making $2.25 for a little Xmas money. Boys left for to spend
    Xmas at home. As a result, I am all alone – as the landlady is going to
    take a holiday tomorrow, I will have to eat out.
December 25
    Christmas Day. All alone. How I miss the family. Tired of sitting in, so
    went to the Grand and saw Jack Oakie in *Sea Legs*. Peculiar I didn't get
    my parcel from home. Spent evening washing clothes, etc.

On December 27th, I started out from London walking toward Hamilton to
meet Alex. With me I took the cake Mother had sent me for Christmas, about all
that I possessed now. I walked 15 miles and slept in the waiting room of the
Thamesville railway station. The next day, I started out again. Hamilton was still
27 miles off. The road was treacherous from the sleet and I kept falling down. I
finally reached Hamilton — only to have Alex tell me of his financial failure. He
was as broke as me!

Alex told me I could sleep in his factory, but, oh what a place — such
gloomy surroundings! I told myself that this sure was starting from the ground up
again if we had gone ahead. I attempted to sleep on one of the top shelves, six
feet from the floor, with my overcoat on for warmth and to soften the bare
boards. I was afraid I would fall off into the shampoo barrels beneath me, so I
decided to spread newspapers out on the floor and lie down alongside the flam-
ing heater, but it was still unbearably cold. I awoke the next day with a bad cough
and my coat covered with splinters from the raw floor boards. No one called with
food and so I had another slice of dear Mother's Christmas cake.

I had never felt so weak and dirty in my life, yet here I was in a soap factory! I
spent a few minutes in prayer, asking God to deliver me out of this terrible mess.
I waited around thinking someone would call. Finally, when no one came by
9:30, I wrote a note to Alex and left it – then picked up my case, locked the door,
and left, walking back towards Toronto.

When I finally reached Toronto, I headed to a Chinese restaurant. It was
one of two on the east side of Church Street. Here I got a full-course meal – soup
to pie – all for 15 cents.

I realized it was going to take a tremendous amount of planning and even
harder work on my part to *survive*, let alone begin to earn any kind of a living.

Events began to deteriorate again and illness set in for me and my room-
mates, John Hensbergen and Jack Andrews, who helped me so much in those
days. I felt so sore and tired that I could hardly walk. Then my diary says that I
heard from Mother:

Pages from Murray's diary for 1930

January 11, 1931

Mother's letter this week helped me so much. Little did they know at home what I was going through those days I was silent in writing. After this, must not forget to write the loved ones who mean so much to me.

January 25

Wrote 26 letters in all today.

February 5

Got a second-hand pair of shoes. Blistered my heels and tore my socks all to blazes. Spent most of the evening darning a skein of yarn into them.

February 6

Came home to find a telegram waiting for me from home saying that a draft for $25 had been sent forward. Really did not know what to do – I was so surprised.

This help from home was intended to give me a new start, which I really appreciated. I began to think how much I would like to be independent and work for myself – start my very own business.

The next eight months were an even greater struggle as I tried, unsuccessfully, to produce and market a product of my own, while continuing to experiment with selling other products.

Another adventure came along in the early fall of 1931. Scotty Graham and Clifford Hicks, from the Chatham area, and Bruce Howard, from Cayuga, joined me as we went back to the "Real Silk Saga" in Western Ontario. Travelling in Scotty's open touring Ford, about 1925 vintage, we left Toronto and barnstormed the Wallaceburg, Chatham, and Dresden areas. The company persuaded us to go up to the Head of the Lakes and cover this virgin territory for them.

We took orders all the way to Sault Ste. Marie, in some of the northern frontier towns, but, when we crossed on the ferry to the American Soo, the border authorities looked at our vehicle and were almost determined to turn us back. Granted it was not very roadworthy, but we "four musketeers" trotted out our best sales pitches, bragged about the old Ford's reputation and swore that there was no reason to suspect that it would falter and break down in the USA.

We skinned through and commenced the long drive through Michigan, Wisconsin, and Minnesota. Most of the nights, we slept in the car. However, one night we were overnight guests of the Eveleth Jail, a spanking new structure, and we were most comfortable.

One morning, our car conked out on the outskirts of a town. The road being downhill, we were able to push it several miles into the town for repairs. In the early morning of the third day, we reached the Minnesota-Ontario border point at Pigeon River around 7 a.m. While the office was open, there were no attendants. After waiting the better part of an hour, we wrote a note, giving full details. We certainly did not want the Michigan Soo officials to get into any trouble for passing us through.

The road to Port Arthur was something else. The fall rains had made it a veritable quagmire. Several times we got stuck and had to shovel and push. Our greatest concern was with the rear wheels. The wooden spokes had become so loose that we were afraid the wheels would collapse. As a safeguard, we finally had to de-tire them and drive spikes through the face of the wheel and into each spoke.

While Scotty frequently was "down" and discouraged, he was the "mudder", while Hicksy was a dandy trooper and used his head at all times. Bruce was out of his element, as he had never faced this kind of hardship before. Nevertheless, he contributed, in his own way, to our wild expedition.

Arriving in Fort William, we were broke. What else was new? We had to find inexpensive accommodations, and selected a place on Simpson Avenue called the Busy Bee Café. Here we got a bed for 25¢ and, in the morning, they served a "Coffee and. . ." for 10¢. This was a plate of bread, rolls, and sometimes a muffin. Usually this held us until evening, when we patronized the Finnish Cooperative Restaurant across the road. Here we could sit down to a groaning table of food, including platters of meat, bowls of vegetables, pitchers of milk – yes, even all the pie you could eat – at a cost of 25¢. All in all, it was quite an experience!

Most of the guests at the Busy Bee "dinged" for a living, and it was interesting to hear their stories. The majority only pursued the trade about one hour a day, usually between 5 and 6 p.m., when they put an arm on the lucky working stiffs as they came out of offices. This objective was usually a dollar in total – sufficient to survive another day.

Our stocking sales were few and far between. Even with the low overhead, we had difficulty in merely surviving. I well remember one day writing up a large order and was already smacking my lips – until I announced my commission, at which time my customer suggested my taking it out in trade. Yes, I had innocently fallen into a house of prostitution. I was later to find out that Mrs. Mathews, affectionately called "Ol' Mag", ran a chain of these houses from her headquarters at 804 Simpson Avenue.

Shortly afterward, Bruce announced to us that his family had sent him sufficient money to go home. My other two buddies threw in the towel, as they could no longer "hack" it. (I cannot remember what happened to the ol' flivver. My hope is that it escaped the "boneyard".)

I stayed on, but that winter in Fort William and Port Arthur was savage. I barely made enough to keep body and soul together. At the end of March, 1932, on a bitterly cold morning, I began to head *east again*.

I took the streetcar to Current River and started walking towards Nipigon, 71 miles away, with $1.10 in my pocket. I walked about 30 miles in all, getting two lifts on the way, then had to give in and spend 60¢ on a train ticket for Nipigon. After indulging in some cookies, this left 25¢.

My clothes were in a wretched condition, aggravated by a headlong slide on a sheet of ice, which tore the knee out of my trousers. I simply had to keep my long – very long – navy blue Elysian cloth overcoat on as a cover-up. I sometimes wonder what I would have done without that coat, though it was becoming quite shabby. It had been given to me by my cousin, Andy Dryden Blair (who was playing hockey for the Toronto Maple Leafs). That night, I borrowed a needle and did my best to repair my trousers knee.

From my diary:
March 30, 1932

> Went down to the skating rink and helped shovel off the snow. A fine bunch of fellows — there is nothing like mixing with people!

April 2

> Arrived in White River at 7:30 a.m. Quite stormy. They pulled a *corpse* out of the locomotive tool box here (I guess freight travel was too slow for the poor devil!).
>
> When I reached Chapleau, I went up some long, narrow stairs into a carpenter's shop, where a CPR man told me I could sleep. Took my shoes and socks off for the first time in almost a week and dried my holey socks over the pipe.

April 3

> This is Saturday and I simply must make some money to live over Sunday since I haven't eaten since in Nipigon on Wednesday.
>
> Received a lovely letter from Mother. She is the dearest mother on earth. Little does she know what I am doing.

I was at a loss to know what to do – to go back west or to continue east. I could not make anything in Chapleau. I started walking to Cartier (140 miles east). At that time there was no Trans-Canada Highway and no road from Nipigon to Chelmsford. The only transportation for that stretch was the railway.

I arrived at Nemogas at 6 p.m., having walked 16 miles on the railway ties. The snow was deep in places and it was heavy walking. I was petered out. I talked to the Station Agent Mr. Henderson, and he suggested I ride a freight. . . .

(I remembered my father talking, one time, about having seen hundreds riding on top of boxcars going through Domain. He had said that a man had to sink to his lowest point to bring himself around to riding a freight train.)

However, I was desperate, and so with Mr. Henderson's help, I clambered aboard with my sample case. What a trip that was on top of that boxcar! In my light topcoat, the wind just pierced me. I tried all sorts of positions, but I had one desperate time to keep from going to sleep and freezing. If it had not been for remembering tips from the book *Arctic Explorations* about survival and the warning signs for which one should be on the lookout, I doubt if I would have come through. I moved up and down the roof of the boxcars, pounding my feet to keep them from freezing, and if I didn't keep my back to the locomotive, the cinders came into my eyes. The 140 miles seemed like 400!

I got off a little outside of Cartier to avoid the CPR constables there. I could hardly stand on my feet. I crawled to the railway YMCA and paid $1 towards a room. It was Good Friday.

I bought a pound of dates with my last 15¢ as I thought they would contain the most food value. I worked 'till 11 a.m. but no luck, so started out walking on

Men rode boxcars at the height of the Great Depression, roaming the country in search of work.

the railway ties again to Chelmsford, 21 miles. It was such a walk. Later, trying to go to sleep, I could still see the railway ties – 2 are too long for 1 step and the ties too close together for one step per tie.

I arrived in Chelmsford at 6 p.m. after six hours of steady walking. The soles were completely gone from my shoes. I replaced my socks again with samples from my case. I was tired and hungry and was still 12 miles from Sudbury, where I might be able to make some money. I just had to get something to eat before starting out. I summoned up enough courage to call at a house to ask for something. A Mrs. Tyne prepared a meal for me and it sure tasted good.

(Many years later I found Mr. Henderson, the Nemogas Station Agent living at Queensville, Ontario, in retirement. He had helped me to get on the freight that first time. I took him an electric blanket as a Xmas gift. Then, in 1946, while on a business trip, I visited the ailing Mrs. Tyne in Sudbury, and we had a long talk. She said she had often wondered what had become of me. Before I left Sudbury, I arranged for flowers to be delivered to that kindly lady. Shortly after I got back to Toronto, I had a letter from her daughter telling me that her mother had passed away. I was so glad I had found her in time. . . .)

April 6, 1932

Easter Sunday. Three miles out of Sudbury. . . almost exhausted so called at the section house and they served me coffee, a couple of eggs and biscuits. . . sure did help.

Got into Sudbury before 1 p.m. and rested my weary dogs in the station. Unable to find a place to sleep so prepared to stay up all night.

April 7

Today I discovered there is a place where the unemployed and men of the road can sleep – in the old jail. I was late finding this out and when I got there it was almost full. Had to go down to the basement. There were hundreds of desperate men in that building. . . it was quite an introduction to life. . . Stayed a whole week, however. Pawned my flashlight today for 35¢ and had a couple of meals of stew for 10¢ each. Had no money left for the weekend.

Then, of all the good luck, I ran into Fred Neil, a neighbour from a farm quite close to ours back west. He coached me on how to successfully ride a freight (not on *top* of the boxcar!)

And so I decided to try my luck again on the freights. After an altercation with the CNR railroad police at MacTier, I rode all the way for free *right into Toronto*, arriving in that city for the second time since leaving home.

MAR. 16. Monday and another miserable day. Snowing very heavily but must work as I haven't a cent in my pocket. Go away out to Westbury tramped away without doing anything. Then went over to West Hamilton & made 1.10, which is a terrible day returns. How discouraging it was tramping around in the mud there being no sidewalks. I'm heartily sick of everything. Tonite but have it to face all again tomorrow. Without a cent in pocket. Have to make rent by Wednesday. May God be with me.

MAR. 17. This may have been a big day for the Irishmen, but it certainly wasn't for me. Made only 1.25. Bewire I am sure I do not know what is going to happen or become of me. Jack came over in evening and left about 10.30 P.M. Have 60 cents in pocket & start morning out in hopes of getting room rent by evening.

MAR. 18. Lively day. Make 3.25 and as a result am able to pay 3.50 rent in evening. Received a lovely long letter from home. Noah I could write a bright cheery one in reply. Spent evening reading and writing.

MAR. 19. Miserable morning. Regular blizzard overhead. How I wish I worked there at all as had only a mere nickel for my breakfast (two oranges). Made 1.50.

fell that hollow spot. Hardly able to walk, but tramped over 6 miles when we came upon a wild raspberry patch — How welcome it was — We first ate & ate and by dark were full of razz-berries & started towards home. Got picked up by a car & arrived at 10 P.M. feeling somewhat better. Terrible thunder storm came up just after we got in & how it poured. Went to bed with just one side touching the mattress at a time instead of two. Paid cheque in morning —

It's mighty early, and over to warehouse for my week's pay. Received $17.60 & was glad to get my hands on it. Had a haircut, clothes press & a new shirt. Bought a flock of groceries almost enough to last the week. Took Bonne-Blue material to Printery and took 5 orders in afternoon. Gnas, did we eat, oh well let's forget all that — In evening went to see about having paddles made & played cribbage with Jack afterwards.

July 7. Worked hard on Hardy — 13 cases. Sore over charging me 2.50 for putting up

CHAPTER THREE

The Budding Entrepreneur

Back in the early days of 1932, when I decided to go into business for myself, I called my company the Dryden Specialty Company. With $25 from home, I went ahead with my dream of going into business, with Ever Bloom plant food as my product. (When I see a specialty company now, I am pretty certain it's a "bedroom operation" as mine was.)

Having tried selling a real variety of items, even to can openers, I would now market my own product house to house. (Imagine selling plant food in the 1930s when food for humans was so hard to come by. . . .)

Back in Hamilton, I bought envelopes and three chemicals and set out to make up 60 packets of Ever Bloom. I advertised for agents to buy the product from me to sell in their own area. Jack Robson, of Hamilton, and I got on very well and sometimes we would go out selling together for mutual encouragement.

Business was discouragingly slow and my diary says that, on February 12th, I started to work with a whole nickel in my pocket and that I hoped it would be

Envelope for Ever Bloom plant food, a product of the Dryden Specialty Company

EVER BLOOM
A NATURAL PLANT FOOD
FOR HOUSE PLANTS AND FERNS

EVER-BLOOM acts as a tonic to plants, in the fact, that it opens the pores of the leaves and flowers, and oxygen feeds the plants in a most natural way.

Directions For Use—(1) Water plants regularly and well. (2) Dissolve one-half teaspoonful of EVER-BLOOM in one quart of water and use not more than once a week.

DRYDEN SPECIALTY CO.

HAMILTON   PRICE 25 CENTS   ONTARIO

BUY NOW AND INSURE PROSPERITY

Business card for Beatty Washers

cold the next day so that my rubbers wouldn't leak. When back in my room, I felt lonely and wrote a long letter home, all the while thinking that I would feel a lot better if I could only phone home. I felt I would like to talk to someone, as it was dreadfully lonesome not knowing anyone in the city except Jack. I wished, too, that I could send money home as they needed it almost as much as I, though they had never mentioned it. Then I pondered how I was going to make the rent without a cent, and I dreaded facing it all again the next day.

There was a hotplate in our room and, after managing a few sales the next day, Jack and I bought canned pork and beans for 11¢, canned spaghetti for 10¢, a loaf of bread for 6¢ and doughnuts for 8¢ – with five coppers left over to buy newspapers. We went home to a "feast" and a good "read", smiling at having outwitted what had seemed like a hopeless predicament.

From my diary:

March 3
> Went to hear Hamilton evangelist Cardy again. Enjoy the singing and feel more comfortable in a place like that in my raggy clothes, than I would in a church.
>
> A person cannot work all the time without something to take the tension off things, so spent a quarter and went and saw Eddie Cantor in *Whoopee* at the Lyric Theatre.

March 5
> The whole day I weigh my chances for making this plant food a success or not. If I don't, I really don't know what will become of me. I am sacrificing everything in an effort to put it over, namely my clothes, eat at cheapest restaurants and spend absolutely no money on amusement.

March 14
> Everything depends on the Gas Bugs (gas saving devices).

March 17
> I am sure I do not know what is going to happen or become of me.

March 24
> Ate 23 small oranges between us, putting in the evening that way. . .

March 31
> Took 1:00 p.m. radial back to Hamilton. . . got card signifying arrival of our Gas Bugs but no money to take them out. . . At 9:30 p.m. Allan Cup game between Winnipeg and Hamilton Tigers was broadcast from Winnipeg Amphitheatre and Winnipeg won 2-1.

April 1
> Fool's Day, and it sure fooled us.

April 2
> Big excitement tonite with Allan Cup match in Winnipeg. Hardly safe for me to live around here, let alone mentioning Wpg. If they win tonite, I certainly will have a lot of fun teasing someone tomorrow. Score 3-1 for Pegs.

April 3
> Ate Hot Cross buns – only way to celebrate Easter.

Mother's watch came in the evening delivery and certainly is very nice.

April 5

Lovely morning – climbed the mountain.

April 6

Our ambition now is to obtain twenty dollars between us so as to get started on the Gas Bug. Oh how we are going to fight towards that end.

Jack and I were back to feeling the effects of undernourishment, and so we signed on as salesmen for Beatty Washers. (If we were having difficulty selling our 25¢ Ever Bloom item, I don't know how we hoped to sell washing machines, but we felt it would be good experience, no matter what happened.)

Before going out on calls, I had to sew my trousers almost every night, but at last was able to "relieve them" by buying new ones. That left me with 10¢ and rent due again.

My diary says that, in early May, I was worrying about how I would phone home for Mother's Day. After I did manage to phone Mother, I wrote: "Just hearing her voice was beautiful. . . ."

May 26

Sold 6 can openers, moth killer & preventive. Washed my one and only shirt.

May 28

First haircut in 5 weeks. Going bareheaded now so will have to keep my head respectable looking.

June 1

Singer Sewing machines.

June 4

Lectured men on selling plant food. Took orders for soft drinks. . .

June 6

Commissions raised to 15¢ a case – $1.05 for 2 days of work.

June 8

Two apples for noon dinner and tried to sell old magazines for my supper.

By June 10th, I had given my landlady my last quarter for the room and there was nothing else to do but go to the Salvation Army Hostel for the night. I was put in a room with three other men . . . another insight into life for me.

June the 22nd to the 29th was a hectic week, according to my diary. I starved most of the time, and every day just managed to make my 25¢ for my bed each night by selling things. I felt dirty but there was nothing but cold water and paper towels.

One night I managed to get some delivery work at the Howdy Beverage warehouse and it was 1 a.m. when I left – too late to get into the Salvation Army Hostel, so I bought a couple of newspapers and went up on the mountainside to sleep. My diary says, "I'd be blowed if I'd part with a dollar for a few hours in a hotel. Laid out the paper and lay on it because the ground was very damp. A cold,

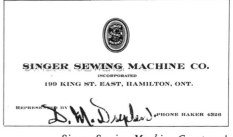

Singer Sewing Machine Company's representative card

Card from Howdy Beverages

raw wind was blowing and I had to lie down bareheaded because I couldn't lie on my straw hat. Lay there for a couple of hours, but it was too cold to sleep. By 3:30 a.m. I got up and walked down to the town."

There I had some doughnuts and coffee in three or four restaurants "and in that manner kicked in the night. . ." (The restaurants mentioned were likely the Bowles Lunch chain, which stayed open all night.)

From the diary again:
July 12
Tested bluing paddles. No article any earthly good unless it can be sold.
July 13
Dispensed hand-bills to 1000 homes. Up early and over to collect my wages – $10.50 for 70 orders. Held 7 or 8 orders back on me, and there is going to be trouble. Almost came to blows over the sink . . . (Howdy)
July 15
Spent whole evening making Bon-E-Blu. Tired, as we as yet have only crude equipment, but it will come in time. Took Jack into camp at cribbage.

Label for Bon-E-Blu, a product of Dryson Manufacturing

DIRECTIONS FOR USING
BON-E-BLU

Stir the Paddle around in the water until the desired shade is produced, then remove Paddle and shake off the few drops which form on the end of it before hanging it up. **NEVER** lay the Paddle down after using. Hang it up, not against the wall, but out at the end of the nail or hook. Be sure to keep the handle of the Paddle out of water. **ALWAYS** stir the water with the hand to distribute the bluing before putting the clothes into the tub. This Paddle is sufficient for 20 or more ordinary washings.

"YOURS FOR SPOTLESS CLOTHES"
Bon-E-Blu
THE BLUING STICK THAT DOES THE TRICK
WORKS LIKE MAGIC

IMPORTANT NOTICE.—Bon-e-Blu will not streak or fleck the clothes. There is nothing to spill or freeze. No bottles to break. No dirty corks to soil the hands or stain the clothes. No bags or balls to bother about. No powders to pester with. Bon-e-Blu does away with them all. And besides, it's superior to any liquid, ball, sheet or powdered bluing in creation. You'll admit that the minute you use it. Use according to directions and you'll be delighted with Bon-e-Blu.

—MANUFACTURED IN CANADA BY—
Dryson Manufacturing Co.
HAMILTON, ONT.

July 16

Mother's birthday. Do hope she got my parcel. Felt like ice cream so went out and got a pint. Ate it before retiring.

July 17

Mrs. Hill, 70 Gage Ave. S. wanted me to try a dish of her raspberry preserves so I did & chatted with her a couple of hours when it was raining.

July 18

Out to sell Bon-E-Blu to make enough to live on over Sunday.

July 19

Went for a hike over the mountain. Walked over 20 miles.

July 23

Applied for $1000 policy – London Life (92¢ on premium for 2 wks.) Feel as though I should carry this with my IOU's.

July 27

Alex called in evening with Silkene sample. Gave it a real good test washing out my silk underwear. Fine stuff. Invited to Mrs. Hill's of Empire Life insurance.

July 28

Up at 6 a.m. to catch up with work. Jacques called saying there was some word of their declining my policy on account of my heart condition.

August 2-4

Civic Holiday. . . on starvation rations. Went down to Bay & saw "Across the Bay" swim contestants come in. Talked soap business. . .

August 5-9

Boarding house – Barnsdale S. Nice home, breakfast & evening dinner – $7.50 per wk. Confederation Life doctor ¾ hr. exam. Heart in bum shape.

There were more weird and wonderful experiences in the '30s in the cosmetics business. While with Canadian Sanitary, we produced several lines which became household words: Hair Kair, Rawson Shampoo, Whizbang After-Shave Lotion, Magic Mask, Masculine Mask, Good Humour Face Lotion, Silkene and Winter Balm.

We merchandised Winter Balm house to house. The salesmen carried one-gallon glass jugs and invited housewives to bring out vessels, into which they would pour samples, leaving a bulk price list for the customer. It was a superb hand lotion and we sold it by the ounce: 3 oz. for 15¢, 6 oz. for 25¢ and 16 ozs. for 50¢.

Winter Balm was a stiff and slow-running material. We surmounted the problem by using hot water bottles. Filled with the hand lotion at the factory, they hung from hooks in the American Austin panel truck. Customers would chuckle when we arrived at the side door with these contraptions – particularly when, with a gentle, under-arm squeeze of the water bottle, the reluctant balm

As representative of Canadian Sanitary, Murray drove a 1933 Austin emblazoned with advertising for the company

MASCULINE MASK - - -
IMPROVES YOUR COMPLEXION

Q.—WHAT IS MASCULINE MASK?

A.—A FACE PACK.

Q.—IS IT OF A CLAY OR MUD NATURE?

A.—NEITHER, IT IS A CREAM. *No mess, muss or stained towels in using it.*

Q.—HOW DO YOU USE IT?

A.—*(1) Wash face with warm water.*
(2) Cover face with coating of Mask.
(3) Allow to set until dry.
(4) Wash off thoroughly with warm water.
(5) Rinse with cold water and wipe dry.

Q.—HOW LONG DOES IT TAKE TO USE IT?

A.—APPROXIMATELY 10 MINUTES.

Q.—HOW DOES IT FEEL ON YOUR FACE?

A.—*First a tingling, then a cooling, and lastly, when set, a tightening, drawing sensation.*

Q.—WHAT WILL IT DO?

A.—*(1) Cleanses the pores.*
(2) Clears the skin.
(3) Helps remove blackheads and pimples.
(4) Refreshes.
(5) Leaves a fragrant, smooth after effect on skin.

Q.—HOW OFTEN SHALL I USE IT?

A.—ONCE TO TWICE A WEEK AS A FACIAL. EVERY DAY LIGHTLY AS AN AFTER SHAVE.

Q.—WHAT IS THE PRICE OF TUBES FOR HOME USE?

A.—(1) SMALL TUBE, 15c; (2) LARGE TUBE, 50c.

Q.—HOW MANY FACIALS IN TUBE?

A.—(1) SMALL TUBE, APP. 3 FACIALS.
(2) LARGE TUBE, APP. 15 FACIALS.

Q.—HOW MUCH DO YOU CHARGE FOR A SHOP TREATMENT?

A.—. . . . . CENTS.

would be drilled into the narrowest-necked medicine bottles.

For barbershops, we had two 20-gallon drums rigged up with hose and faucet connection, similar to a gas pump. We sold on the bulk principle. Every barbershop had quart bottles left over from hair preparations. Transfer was simple. We would take an empty bottle out to the car, set it on the sidewalk, whip out the hose, fill the container and collect 40¢.

We reached the stage where a wave set should be added to our line. Coming up with a promising product which had all the important selling ingredients – colour, perfume, package, etc. – necessary for maximum sales potential, the question of a suitable name proved a stumbling block. I told Alex that I had named most of our other products and felt that he should put a product name on this one.

Alex replied that he had an idea, and went on to say, "Do you remember Helene Flach? Well, since I came back from the west, she has hardly given me the time of day. She thinks I'm a drifter and, for months, has refused to go out with me. What do you say we call it Helene Wave Set?"

I told him that I liked it, so when the first 16-ounce bottle came off the assembly line, a handsome embossed label was put on it. Alex stuck it under his arm and headed up the mountain to see Helene. He had decked himself out in his navy blue suit, overcoat with black velvet collar and his black bowler. Upon his return, he proclaimed, "She *loved* it, especially our calling it after her! *I'm in like a duck*!"

The traffic up that mountain in Hamilton got heavier and heavier. However, the courting intensity got a setback while Alex was out of town for a couple of weeks. Arriving back at the factory, he inquired if I had had any reports or feedback on the new wave set. I told him that I hadn't, but that sales were booming. Wondering why he had asked, I was told, "I saw Helene uptown and I know she saw me, BUT she passed with her nose in the air – I just wondered. . . ."

Well, the next day a telephone call came from an irate hairdresser. She had sold a bottle to one of her customers who lived in Westdale. This customer had been experiencing plumbing problems, and evidently the plumber had had to make a return trip and she'd had to pay him a second time. She warned him that if it still wasn't satisfactory, the next trip would be on him. He had barely reassured her and driven away when there was a loud crash in the bathroom! She immediately telephoned the plumber to get back and to fix the problem properly.

Upon returning, he checked and found the plumbing in order; however, he noticed something trickling down from the medicine cabinet above the sink. Upon opening it, he noted that "all hell had broken loose!" One of our bottles of wave set had exploded, smashing most of the bottles on the shelf. The customer, of course, had to pay the plumber again. Naturally she was holding the hairdresser responsible for the plumber's charges, plus reimbursement for the explosion damages.

It turns out that we had neglected to include a preservative, like salicylic acid, and the stuff worked and worked within the bottle, thinning out like water, the colour fading to a sickly gray, and giving off the smell of rotten eggs. To make matters worse, there was no record of these sales to help us trace which customers to telephone in order to call the product in. Many of the bottles exploded during the night, bringing us even greater embarrassment. This "goof" not only rocked the fortunes of our cosmetics business, but terminated a beautiful romance.

Murray dressed in his best, Hamilton, 1933

Thinking back to those days in Hamilton, I remember the pawn shop at the corner of King William and Mary streets, where I pawned my clothes – piece by piece – during the '30s. One item, a beautiful wine-and-gray dressing gown, which had been given me by a lady friend one Christmas, went for a magnificent $1.25.

Not only was our advertising a sign of our immaturity, so were the surface things we did to belie our age. My cover-up was a disastrous attempt to grow a moustache. Being very blonde, and possessing a sparse beard, I had difficulty sprouting a 'stache that showed.

Pencilling was tried but only added phoniness, so someone suggested sodium nitrate. Armed with a small bottle of this, I daubed the faintly discernible whiskers liberally, getting much of it off-target and ending up with what appeared to be a dirty face. Lemon, pumice . . . these, too were tried but they only

Murray's light moustache was grown to give him a mature look; he later removed it to look younger.

added to my problems and eventually gave me scabs. (Believe it or not, I lived with that upper lip foliage for thirty-seven years – until one day the thought suddenly struck me: if I grew it originally to make myself look older, then I should now remove it to make myself appear younger! Off it came.)

During the period we were in the cosmetics business, I spent considerable time on Ontario roads, calling on barbershops and beauty parlours. In 1935, at Parkhill, I had a serious car accident.

I was driving down the main street, around 11:30 a.m., keeping my eyes peeled for barber pole signs, when, all at once, there was a crash – and a boy's body went hurtling through the air, falling on the hood of the Austin and then slipping off onto the street and barely missing the hind wheels. The boy was bleeding badly and crying, "I'm dying, I'm dying!"

At this point, someone came up to me and asked, "Have you got insurance?" Needless to say, I was devastated. An urgent call was made for a priest to administer the last rites.

The only doctor in town had just gone out to a harvest field to attend someone involved in a threshing-machine accident. When he returned, he did what he could but instructed that the lad, Hugh Larkin, be taken into London – some thirty-five miles away– to hospital. As there was no ambulance, he had to be taken by car.

I was in a complete daze when a Mr. Fred Brewer, who ran the local hardware store, took me to his living quarters above the store. There he and his wife gave me a comfortable place to lie down and a cup of tea.

Many people had witnessed the accident, and a few of them reconstructed what had happened. The boy had attempted to make a right turn coming off a stop street and, instead of hugging the curb, had sailed out into the main street, hitting my left front fender. When his body came to rest, it was a few inches over on my side of the road.

When the Ontario Provincial Police came in and measured the road to obtain the necessary information, they said that they would have to hold me and take me to London. There a full report was made out. When finished, the officer, Inspector Wharton, pronounced, "Well, it is about 50-50." I inquired as to where I was at fault. He hemmed and hawed, then stuttered and said, "Well, we will make it 60-40. You know, what we say is usually accepted by the Court." As a 24-year-old, I tell you my respect for Canadian justice plummeted!

The next morning, my case was brought up in court. I was charged, under the Highway Traffic Act, with "hitting a boy on a bicycle while in charge of driving a car," and was held on $4000 bail. As the Larkin boy was hovering between life and death, the case had to be remanded. I did not have anything approaching the amount of bail, and so I had to go back to jail.

Two days later, on a Saturday morning – the busiest day in their store – Mr. and Mrs. Fred Brewer drove into London, posted the bail, and had me released. The Brewers invited me back to convalesce with them. During that period I visited Hugh Larkin a few times in hospital. He fully recovered after six weeks and the case proceeded in Court. The charge was read, following which the Crown

Attorney got up and said, "Instead of the car striking the bicycle, the bicycle struck the car. I withdraw the charge and dismiss this case." If it hadn't been for the fine Christian act of the Brewers, I could have languished in that horrible jail for six weeks.

I had been taught that, under our judicial system, one is considered innocent until proven otherwise. This experience, to me, had proven exactly the opposite.

This story of my early entrepreneur days would be incomplete, and I would be remiss, if I neglected to relate a serious incident that happened in Hamilton in the '30s.

Among other sales endeavours at that time, I worked for the Hamilton Automobile Club, of the Ontario Motor League, selling memberships on a commission basis. Struggling to keep alive, I foolishly used some of the money collected for OML memberships and converted it towards room rent and food. Always optimistic – to a fault – I kept saying to myself that next week, next month, things would be better and I would be able to straighten the record. It didn't happen, and the constant gnawing worry of having done this wrong only served to jeopardize my health and to devastate my abilities to earn.

Finally, distraught and almost cornered, I went to see the Manager, Mr. Cal Davis, and confessed the terrible thing that I had done. While he was shocked, he was most understanding. We worked out a plan for reimbursement and, over a considerable period of time, I was able to repay this $65 conversion of funds. This was another critical time in my life. Again I was fortunate to have the help and understanding of a Christian gentleman. Had I not, I could easily have acquired a criminal record. Calvin Davis, may your soul rest in peace. . . .

In the '30s, Alex Hilson and I decided to get together again for another effort via the Styptic Pencil route. We had a set of moulds made up, then cranked out the pencils and labelled them. We inserted them in glass vials, displaying a dozen on a card and selling them to barbershops, where they were retailed for 15¢ each. Before we could afford this inventory outlay, we had built up our financial position by barnstorming some of the small towns and villages, selling to individuals.

When we hit a centre, Alex would insist that I call on all the Chinese restaurants and laundries. I seemed to have empathy with the Chinese, although they are, possibly, the toughest nation in the world to sell. As I had a few adolescent pimples on my face, I would pull out all the stops, jambing the styptic into the "claret" of a pimple after having removed the top of it. It was almost a sure sale! (Remember that, in those days, a large segment of the shaving population still shaved with the old straight razor, which meant more lacerations. . . and more styptics to stop the flow of blood!)

I had continued my selling during the early World War II years, but by spring of 1942 I made up my mind to get into some sort of service for my country. That service ended in early 1946, and I went back to my civilian career.

Murray with Dr. Sid Albin of the Albin Institute of Physical Health, 1936

Murray's card from the Albin Institute

CHAPTER FOUR

Hamilton and Marriage

I had begun to settle down somewhat to life in Hamilton by 1937. I became a member of the Badminton Club at my church, First United. One Saturday afternoon, while I was playing, Margaret Moffat came up to me to say that she had been trying to contact me all week to invite me to a dinner party that she was having that night (30 January 1937). I said that I was sorry but that I had other plans for the evening. I had asked Ethel Primer to go dancing with me. Still, I was disappointed. . . .

Around 4 p.m., while playing a singles match and racing across the court to return a shot, my right heel caught on a loose board in the floor, causing me to twist my ankle. My ankle swelled up almost immediately and caused me a lot of pain. I certainly could no longer dance. I telephoned Ethel to tell her about it and I remember saying, "You know what a lousy dancer I am on two feet, let alone attempting it on one." So we cancelled that date. Of course I was not too crippled to attend a dinner party! I was able to get the invitation renewed.

It was there that I met Margaret Campbell, a friend of Margaret Moffat, who was visiting her for the weekend. Very soon after, I was to get her address and to make the first overture! Later on, after our marriage, we attended First United Church and visited that north badminton court, fastening our eyes on the repaired floorboard while thinking what an insignificant piece of wood had meant to our lives. When that fine old Hamilton monument was destroyed by fire years later, we felt a real sense of loss.

Our first date was 18 February 1937. We went to a hockey game at Maple Leaf Gardens. A cousin of mine, Syl Apps, put on a great show for us that night.

Margaret was assistant in charge of the Model Kindergarten School of Toronto Normal, at that time located on Gould Street. My courting could hardly be classified as whirlwind, as I found the trip to Toronto too expensive to go at every whim. Driving home late at night, via the Lakeshore (before the Queen Elizabeth Way was built), I was usually dangerously groggy by the time I reached Oakville. By trial and error I finally found that three quarters of a bottle of Coke would keep me wide-eyed until I reached Hamilton, and yet I was ready for sleep when I hit the bed.

Murray with Margaret at Larimac Links cottage in the Gatineau, 1937

Telegram confirming the engagement of Margaret and Murray

CANADIAN NATIONAL TELEGRAM

D. E. GALLOWAY, ASSISTANT VICE-PRESIDENT, TORONTO, ONT.

FORM 6124

CLASS OF SERVICE	SYMBOL
Full-Rate Message
Day Letter	DL
Night Message	NM
Night Letter	NL

If none of these three symbols appears after the check (number of words) this is a full-rate message. Otherwise its character is indicated by the symbol appearing after the check.

Exclusive Connection with WESTERN UNION TELEGRAPH CO. Cable Service to all the World Money Transferred by Telegraph

RA505 46 NL

STANDARD TIME 1938 JUL 22 PM 9 37

HAMILTON ONT 22

MISS MARGARET CAMPBELL

CARE J R BINKS GATINEAU POWER CO VICTORIA BLDG OTTAWA ONT

PULLING A MAHATMA ON ME EH IN FORM OF LETTER FAST STOP CAVIAR TOES
WITH EGG PLANT REMAINDER OF WEEK STOP OUR FONDEST HOPES DEAR CAN BE
PLANNED FOR SEPT ANYTIME STOP WANTED YOU TO KNOW FOR WEEKEND HENCE
THIS WIRE STOP AM WRITING MUCH LOVE

MURRAY.

For Prompt Service - Call
2-3535
Cor. Sparks and Metcalfe Streets

FORM 6124

It got to be amusing for, when I entered The Modern Café, the only restaurant open, the owner, Len Guey, would automatically go to the big red cooler for my Coke.

As Margaret and her widowed mother got to know me and my intentions better, I was invited to stay over Saturday nights in their duplex at 37 Hawthorne in Rosedale. Car parking was a problem in that area but the short wheel base on my little Willys Coupe allowed me to nose up to the living room bay window and just clear the sidewalk.

During the first summer, I was invited down to Margaret's aunt and uncle's cottage at Larimac Links on the Gatineau River. The air down there was pretty "heady" stuff and, one moonlight night, following a dance, I plighted my troth in the dark confines of the Binks' frame garage. On 11 September 1937, just before departing for the CNE to dance to the music of Guy Lombardo, I presented Margaret with her engagement ring. While I really could not afford it, I nevertheless wanted to substantiate my claim and to declare a "hands off" signal to any other aspirants. I had visited People's Credit Jewellers in Hamilton, selecting a modest diamond. The price was $100, with $5 down and $1 per week. I almost did not qualify for credit as they insisted on everything but a saliva test. Having to give Margaret's name and address was most embarrassing.

Many a week I had to do some tall scratching to dig up the dollar payment, and I breathed a lot easier when I made the final payment just prior to purchasing the wedding ring. When I presented the ring to Margaret on that memorable evening, I apologized for the "minute-ness" and promised I would trade it in on something more worthy of her at a later date. She was horrified that I should ever make such a suggestion. Everywhere, she showed it off proudly to friends and her "bubbliness" greatly pleased me.

In subsequent months, I avoided the wedding date topic because I plain could not afford it. While I had always said that I would not marry until I had $5000 in the bank, I had long since given up that unattainable target, but I did not wish to have financial worries immediately following the wedding.

May came and a decision had to be made as Margaret would have to notify the Toronto School Board if she was not planning to return in the fall.

It seems almost ludicrous now as I write this, but a friend owed me $100 – I went to him, discussed the matter and asked him if, should I decide to get married in September, I could count on the money. I needed it for our wedding trip, which would take the form of a motor trip out to my parents' Manitoba farm. It would not be expensive – merely the cost of gas plus maybe six nights on the road to and from. He assured me that I could count on the $100.

I recall that I then dropped into Hainsworth Drugs at Main and Fairholt, ordered a Coke at the fountain and worded a telegram to Margaret.

We set a 17 September 1938, date. It was to be a small evening wedding to be held in the Campbells' home.

Business was not good and sales reached such a low level that I worried more than ever. It was impossible to get a few dollars ahead. And then everything tumbled around my ears when, two weeks before the wedding, I received the shocking news that the $100, or any part thereof, could not be paid before the 17th. This placed me in an alarming situation. I had counted heavily on this and, without it, would not have enough funds to carry us to the US border. In desperation, I went to see the bank manager, Mr. Hall, at the Bank of Commerce, Holton and King streets, where I had my meagre account. In those days, the glass door was always closed.

After hearing the full details, Mr. Hall's reply was, "You have only one option: postpone the wedding." When I told him that the invitations had all gone out, and that the wedding must go on, he raised himself from the swivel chair and escorted me to the door. Passing some advertising material in racks in the lobby, I called back, "What about these personal loans?" "You could not qualify, being merely a commission agent," he retorted. Still grasping at straws, I added, "But if I can get a guarantor?" He reluctantly agreed that, if I could procure someone of substance, I might have a chance, but I almost had to plead for the necessary forms.

Armed with the forms, I contacted Ida Tofflemire, who covered the Hamilton news for the *Toronto Star*'s "Over the Teacups" column. She gladly signed it, although she got paid not on what she wrote but on what the *Star* used. As I was sure this would not impress a hard-headed banker, I then got in touch with Jimmie Allen, a young man of around thirty and whom I did not know too well. He did, however, work steadily at the Steel Company of Canada. Understanding my position, he also willingly signed the application for $130, with repayment monthly with interest over a period of eighteen months.

When I took the completed forms in to Mr. Hall, he perused the names of the guarantors but certainly did not act impressed. As I was leaving, I inquired as to when I might come back for a "reading". He replied, "No use of your coming in here. You will be notified by head office in Toronto." After about a week, my nerves started to bother me as I kept looking for mail, pro or con.

Ten days went by and, only a few days before the wedding, I returned to the bank. Mr. Hall was annoyed at my bothering him. "I told you there was no use coming back here as we receive no progress report on requests for loans." I had reached the mental state where my work began to deteriorate, and I ate very little as my stomach was in such turmoil. Every morning and afternoon, I would check for mail with Mrs. Wilkins, my landlady at 34 Barnesdale. I prayed earnestly on the matter but I could never bring myself around to explaining it all to Margaret. While I was sure she knew that she was not marrying a rich man, I was equally sure she was not about to marry a pauper.

Gavin Young gave me a fine stag party, but my heart was not in it. Many times since, I have been a guest at such parties and envied the groom-to-be as he revelled in his pre-nuptial events. Even the lovely mixed parties given for us, I couldn't enjoy.

Plans had been made for a rehearsal on the night before the wedding. What a worrisome trip it was that night! Long afterwards, Margaret said that I looked like "death warmed over" and that she wondered if I would be able to make my own wedding.

34 Barnesdale in Hamilton

Wedding picture of Margaret and Murray

Saturday morning dawned. In those days, we got eleven postal deliveries a week, including one on Saturdays. It was my final chance! I drove my little 1933 Ford down Barnesdale, almost to King Street, parked and sat waiting for the postman. When he came along, I got out of the car and inquired if he had any mail for me. He went down deep into his bundle, extracting a long envelope with a window front, above which was printed Canadian Bank of Commerce. In those days, a window envelope meant only one thing – a cheque! As the postie handed it to me, I went berserk – hugging and, yes, I think even kissing him. I'm sure he thought me mad. Inside was my cheque for $130. I had been saved by a narrow margin of eight hours! Later on, there was difficulty meeting those eighteen monthly payments, but they were made without in any way jeopardizing the two kind people who had come to my rescue.

Margaret's mother provided a lovely wedding, and Margaret never looked more beautiful than when we pronounced our vows in a seven o'clock candlelight ceremony. Dr. George Williams, a Welsh friend of the family, officiated. My best man was Dr. Morley Whillans. Several times since, I have kidded Margie that I really am not sure about actually being married because I hardly understood a word he said.

The small, select group of guests gave us a warm send-off. When we reached Brantford and the Bodega Hotel, where we had reservations, we phoned Mother and, typically, I had to use Margie's money for the pay phone.

Our trip west through the United States was delightful, as we motored in September sunshine each day. One afternoon, we stopped by a highway patrol cruiser to request information. The officer relayed an exciting message that he had just received in his vehicle. Chamberlain had met Hitler at Munich and announced "peace in our time".

Needless to say, we got a warm welcome on reaching home! I was so dawgone proud to show off my bride to family and friends. Everybody loved her.

As we left, Mother and Dad gave us forty dollars and this saved our skins, because we ran into a bit of trouble with the car on the way back.

In Hamilton, we had leased, for $40 a month, an upper duplex for one year at 180 London Street South. Mother Cambpell had given up the Toronto duplex and moved into a flat in Hamilton, too. We were most fortunate to acquire her excess furniture for our modest apartment.

My work continued to be unsettled. For a period of several months, two other chaps joined me in a classified advertising newspaper project. We approached publishers of weekly newspapers and contracted to sell a six-month classified advertising programme for them on a commission basis.

The weekly page was headed "Where to shop in. . . ." We contacted businesses in the town, prepared suggested copy for their advertisement and had them sign 26-week contracts. While not the most lucrative business endeavour, it was a wonderful experience.

The publishers were happy and surprised at how we obtained advertising contracts from sources that they had never been able to crack. Some of the towns we covered were Elmira, Tillsonburg, Aylmer, Waterloo, Delhi, and Fort Erie ("Where to shop in Buffalo"). However, at best it was a "stopgap" type of endeavour. Remuneration was uncertain, and it was always difficult financing ongoing expenses until the completion of each programme, when we got paid.

It was a rough way to start married life. It was a whole new world for Margaret. As a teacher on a fixed income, she had always been a careful budgeter. My hit-and-miss financing was cruel to her and she worried a lot. My pride hit rock-bottom when I discovered that she was doing some baking on the side and supplying a small shop on Ottawa Street.

We could not afford to renew our London Street lease but were able to locate a smaller duplex at 122 Garrick Avenue for $32.50 a month. The kitchen was so small that only one could work in it at a time.

In the fall of 1940, I got a position with C.W. Vincent, ecclesiastical tailors, calling on the clergy. My territory was all over Ontario. It was pleasant work, as I called on clergy of all denominations. I measured them for gowns, cassocks, clerical and business suits.

I thoroughly enjoyed dealing with the "Members of the Cloth" because they were so friendly and hospitable. . . I always had to stay for lunch or dinner with them. While a radical departure from anything I had ever done, I was reasonably successful and our financial picture did improve.

* * *

Before we were married, Margaret promised to do everything in her power to help me in my work. However, knowing the Dryden penchant for getting involved in public life, she warned me that if I ever made a move towards the political arena, she would walk straight out. She kept her word and I kept mine!

* * *

A few weeks before our 25th Wedding Annversary, I called on the people living in Margaret's old abode at Hawthorne Avenue, Rosedale. I mentioned that we had been married in their living room almost a quarter century before, and

Murray reunited with the old plough during honeymoon visit to the Domain farm

180 London Street South, Hamilton

122 Garrick Avenue, Hamilton

wondered if they would mind our family visiting them come 17 September (1963) at 7 p.m. I felt that my wife and her mother would love to visit their old home again, and that our three children were equally interested. We received a warm invitation and, on the appointed evening, we had dinner at the Boulevard Club and arrived at the Hawthorne Avenue home sharp at 7:00. It was a great thrill, and the occupants were so kind and thoughtful in showing us around. We then went on to the Royal Alexandra and saw *Never Too Late*. All in all, it was an anniversary to remember.

Claude W. Vincent was one of Murray's employers in the early 1940s: card, catalogue, cloth sample

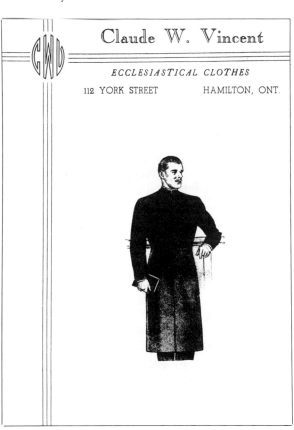

The War Years

In the early spring of '42, I finally did what I had wanted to do for more than six months. The war, while still more or less static insofar as Canada was concerned, was beginning to show ugly signs of an all-out world conflagration. By no stretch of the imagination was I engaged in an essential industry. The closest I came in my line of work was in restricting my customers to purchasing the new-fangled "Victory" suit, (no cuffs, no vest, no watch-pocket, one pair of pants only) and so I gave notice to my employer and resigned.

I visited RCAF headquarters in Hamilton, procuring data, and in the afternoon I dropped down to the badminton club at the church. There I renewed acquaintance with Alf Morris, who was home on weekend leave from #31 RAF at Collins Bay where he was serving the YMCA. When he heard of my plans, he asked "Why don't you visit the YMCA war services headquarters?" I replied that I did not think I could qualify. He disagreed, saying that he knew my capabilities and was also familiar with the requirements for the position.

Before I left he extracted a promise that I would call Mr. Manley Chisholm for an appointment and interview. I followed through on the Monday, made an appointment and, following the interview, took away the application and examination forms.

In a matter of about three weeks I was accepted and sent to the RCAF station at Aylmer, Ontario for basic training. Later I was transferred to Camp Borden for further training, where I specialized in regimental sports. I thoroughly enjoyed the work.

In early October I was posted as Senior Supervisor to Barriefield Camp at Kingston, where some 7000 troops were in training. Here we had a diversified and expansive programme. I worked with three other supervisors covering administration, sports and entertainment. A lot of our work consisted in tapping and harnessing the help of local community organizations. The citizens of Kingston responded enthusiastically and supported many of the activities at the Barriefield Recreation Centre. It was a 7-day-a-week programme, and the hut was open from 8 a.m. to usually near midnight.

The dances were, of course, the most popular form of entertainment. Girls from Kingston were brought in by bus. Those who didn't have tickets for the dance that particular night would be lined up, gazing longingly as the lucky ones greeted the girls in excited fashion and headed into the Recreation Hall for the big dance.

Murray in YMCA uniform

*On leave, with Dave, at home in
Hamilton, 1943*

To make the floors more "dance-able", borax powder was sprinkled on ahead of time. The floor eventually became so worn that the knots stood out like warts, which were uncomfortable on the feet. If they were of knotty pine, they were well named.

It was difficult for me to get home often, so we decided to rent a cottage for August at nearby Dead Man's Bay. It was quite a month for the four of us. David was almost two years of age. Conveniences were practically non-existent, and Margie's stories of that month get better with each telling. No lights, no water, outside plumbing and about two miles to shopping. . . .

One night a group of German prisoners-of-war escaped from Fort Henry, less than half a mile from our cottage. I had difficulty making my way home late that night as the strong searchlights practically blinded me. Upon my arrival, **Mother and Margaret were almost in a state of petrifaction, as security forces kept the frame cottage under constant surveillance.**

One night, back in April, a private had turned in a telegram to me. It was addressed to his wife in Galt and the message read: "Will be home on Saturday night." For this he paid 37¢ out of his $1.30 daily pay. The thought came to me that, undoubtedly, other troopers had telephoned Galt that night and would have been glad to pass on the information.

After closing the hut, I went to my barracks room, got into bed, sipped on a glass of water (most would have had a cigarette), and pondered the problem. It seemed that every time I plugged a hole, a leak would break out some place else. A couple of times I almost gave up, but the solution seemed so close. Just before 3 a.m., I had the formula and then I was so excited I couldn't sleep a wink! I wanted to get over to the Officers' Mess as soon as it opened to spring it on our legal officer. While he liked it, he couched his legalese with words of caution. He naturally wondered about the Bell Telephone Company's reaction.

The following morning, I went into Kingston to have a talk with Mr.

Kierstead, the Bell manager. He was most impressed, gave it his blessing, and even offered to supply telephone directories for Toronto, Hamilton and Montreal, the three cities where we considered operating. I drafted a message form and had it mimeographed. We called the idea the "YMCA Message Service". The message form asked for the name, telephone number, relationship to recipient, the message and, finally, the sender's name. We advertised: "10 words for 10 cents", and a penny for each extra word. We publicized it in DRO's (Daily Routine Orders) and the first night we had forty-eight messages.

Ralph Bates, one of our supervisors, arranged for his wife, Joan, to accept the messages in Toronto because she could handle shorthand. I bought a photographic timer. At seven o'clock sharp, I put a station-to-station call through and Joan was waiting by the telephone. I would give her the messages and, as our line charges were 58¢ for three minutes or approximately 20¢ a minute, we had to bang through two messages a minute to break even. As soon as we completed all the messages, Joan or the other volunteer operators would relay the messages.

Ken Dryden tries on his dad's hat and trousers around 1951

The messages usually went like this: "Mrs. Smith, this is the YMCA Message Service and we have a message from your husband Jack in Barriefield." Joan Bates would proceed to give the message, then hang up and call the next one, until all were delivered. In a matter of days, we extended the service to Montreal through the Triangle Club, and to Hamilton where Margaret did the honors. The story appeared in the Kingston *Whig-Standard* and was then picked up by Canadian Press.

At this point our troubles started. A Bell Telephone executive appeared and wanted all the details, which I furnished. The service grew, like Topsy, to the point where we were processing over 500 per week. We added a "Return Message Service". After completing our outgoing messages, we would ask for the incoming messages. We furnished the camp personnel with the volunteer operators' telephone numbers so that messages could be left any time during the day. Upon receiving these return messages, we had runners who took them out and pinned them on the soldiers' beds.

Claire Wallace did a feature during one of her programmes, and again more Bell officials landed on our doorstep. I tried to explain to them that, in this particular camp, most of the troops did not know, until the last minute, if they had a weekend leave. It would then be too late to write and too expensive to phone. Anyway, every night there was usually a long line-up in front of the pay telephones. I also reminded them that we were paying full line charges, barely broke even, and some nights – on bum connections – we went in the hole.

We added a further service and called it "Telemoney Service", where we transferred small amounts of money in emergencies. The "Canadian Cavalcade" programme interviewed one of our Toronto volunteer operators, Marion Corlett. These volunteers, even one bed-ridden lady in Toronto, enjoyed the work while getting a good feeling of doing something for our forces. They kept little notebooks, saw little romances commence, sometimes bloom, oftentimes fade. When a wife or a girlfriend didn't get a message by 8 p.m., she would call the volunteer and inquire.

Margaret Dryden receiving phone service messages at Hamilton for relay to wives and sweethearts of soldiers at Barriefield

ENCLOSE THIS IN YOUR LETTER

Y.M.C.A. <u>RETURN</u> MESSAGE SERVICE

If you wish to send a message to your soldier boy in Barriefield Camp — phone the Depot Number listed below before 7 p.m. week-days, and 4.30 p.m. Sundays. Leave the message (10 words maximum). We will pick it up on our regular nightly call, deliver it and collect the 10c charge at this end.

DEPOT NUMBERS

Toronto -		Montreal - Plateau 8739
Hamilton -	2-1875	Ottawa -

NAME AND REGIMENTAL NUMBER **MUST** ACCOMPANY ALL MESSAGES

Again, I had two of the Bell higher echelon pay me a lengthy visit. At this juncture I had found my patience wearing very thin. I posed this question to them. "What is the matter with it?" Their answer: "We don't like it." I said, "Will you put that in writing?" They refused (and never once later did they correspond). I said, "Well, that is just too bad. There happen to be over 7000 in this camp and I dare say there is not one of us here because we like it."

I added that I had reached the end of my tether, and that I had the full support of the Camp Commander. The latter had gone on record that the service was a great morale booster for the camp, as loved ones could be alerted to meet trains and ailing ones could be reassured. At this point, I looked my visitors square in the eye and said: "If you attempt to stop this service, I will bootleg the calls. If this fails, our car is sitting up off its wheels in the garage at home. I am prepared to sell it and put a full-page advertisement in a daily newspaper telling the complete story."

They knew I meant business, and I called off the news media because every release made the Company nervous. From then on we encountered no further trouble, although the Canadian National Telegraph manager informed me that they, Bell, had attempted to enlist their support. CN shied away from that, saying it was a dynamite issue and would only serve to damage their public relations. In reality, if the service was hurting anyone, it was the telegraph firms.

In the period in which we operated, over 15 000 messages were processed. I still recall some of the cute ones: "Coming home on Friday night, put two on ice" and, "Coming home for the week-end, please arrange date with Gloria Pearlman or reasonable facsimile."

I always regretted this hassle with the Bell Company because I have been, and still am, one of their strong allies. Editorially, I have been in their corner when tussling with the Department of Transport for rate increases, or when unthinking people tried to start a movement to nationalize the telephone system (and have it run like the Post Office? – God forbid!). The Bell was clearly misguided at Barriefield. During the same period, full-page Bell advertisements were appearing in national publications patting themselves on the back for their war effort. It all seemed inconsistent at the time.

During 1943, at Barriefield Camp, one of many overseas drafts went out. The troops were allowed to send one ten-word telegram. For security reasons, the wording had to be carefully "couched". While the majority of the messages followed a pattern and many indulged in a bit of self-pity, there was one message that, over the span of forty years, I have remembered word for word. It read "Keep the home fires burning and remember to keep smiling." While I have long since forgotten his name, I can still see him – a tall, blond, good-looking NCO from Winnipeg. His farewell message expressed such deep concern for his wife. I hope he made it back.

After eighteen months in Kingston, I was anxious for an overseas posting. However, the area supervisor, Jack Norman, wanted me to do a stint at the RCAF Instrument Flying School, Deseronto. I was terribly upset and felt I was being passed by. He promised that if I would go down there and straighten out their problems, he would grant my wish in six months. He kept his word, too, and I was never sorry for this challenge at Deseronto. It was a great station, and I was almost sorry to leave.

I asked the MO, Flight-Lieutenant John Wright, if he would give me a health recommendation, but he wouldn't. He said, "Don't ask me to do anything like that because you know as well as I do that your 'ticker' is malfunctioning." Later at the Horse Palace (at Canadian National Exhibition Place) in Toronto, I went through each phase of the overseas medical examination lickety-split until I came to the heart phase. There, everyone wanted to listen as they passed the stethoscope around. They called in Colonel John Hepburn, the heart specialist, and after a good listen he huddled with the MOs. I heard the Colonel say, "I won't let him go," and with that I almost "blacked out". The Colonel came over to me and rendered his decision. I tried to reason with him that I had had the condition all my life. (In fact, insurance companies had always rated my premiums upward twelve to fourteen years.) It hadn't hampered me and should not be affected in this branch of the service, but he was not impressed.

Just as I was losing the battle, an officer, whom I thought I recognized, went by the doorway. I asked if Colonel M. James was there. He said, "Yes". I then asked permission to see him as he knew me and my work from Barriefield. I discussed the matter with Colonel James at length, and he in turn huddled with Colonel Hepburn. The result: I passed my medical!

In less than two weeks I was on my way to Windsor, Nova Scotia and on to the steamship *Pasteur*. After a couple of weeks' training in Aldershot, England, I was posted to Italy, travelling there on an old tub, the *Scythia*. I often wondered why I was sent over there as my duties were menial in Avelino and Texas, a camp just outside Naples. I was shunted back north, landing at Marseilles, France, and then convoyed up through France and into Holland. I was in Nijmegen on the night of the liberation, celebrating the event at the #3 Canadian General Hospital party.

Murray's farewell to Deseronto Camp,
November 1, 1944

The Siesta Club in Hilversum, Netherlands, 1945

Shortly after the capitulation, I was asked to set up a small club in Hilversum, Holland. We were able to obtain a large house and commenced a limited programme, plus a canteen operation that we named the Siesta Club.

After two months, Auxiliary Headquarters requested that I immediately attempt to locate a larger building in the same city. As Hilversum was essentially a residential city with a modest 100 000 population, it was not easy to find a suitable building for our purpose. The Public Library was about our only possibility. The Nazis had taken it over and used it as a Mess and, believe you me, they had hurriedly left it in a mess. The library authorities were naturally anxious to get it back functioning again as a library. However, cognizant of our problem, they were agreeable to our using it for a short while.

Before going ahead with any construction and maintenance, we decided to call in the Chairman of the Board and also an architect. They accompanied us on a tour of the building. We wanted to cooperate and promised that any structural change should be made with the thought in mind that, in a few months, the structure would revert to library use. After the tour, the chairman inquired if I had a contractor in mind. He suggested one whose name was Seppen. We made up a contract and gave him the "go ahead". When a week had elapsed, with very little activity outside of the appearance of one carpenter, and a painter daubing a bit of paint here and there, I called Seppen in and told him we were not happy with the progress. He replied that it was difficult to procure tradesmen because many of them were engaged in black market activities, but he added, "Not to worry," he would complete the job inside of six weeks. "*Six weeks!*" I cried, "We all hope to be home in that time. I will give you six days."

He replied, "It is impossible." I was desperate at this point. Army Headquarters was on our backs. The several thousand troops in the area, with nothing to do, were causing considerable problems with the civilians. I decided to go out to Laarn and see the Commandant at the Collaboration Camp and enlist his help in supplying prisoners as workers. At first, he would not even consider it. He was afraid that we would treat them too kindly. Too, he was worried about the security. When I agreed to *their* posting of guards, we came to terms.

The following morning, we went out with two 60-hundredweights. Every prisoner wanted to come. They would sidle up to me and brag about their

Murray and hosts, the Huenders, at the billet in Hilversum

Murray in jeep he named after his wife, 1945

Murray in his billet bed in the Huenders' home

capabilities, saying things like: "Take *me*. Before the war I was the largest tile contractor in all Holland." So severely treated, they were anxious to get out of the camp environment for a few hours. We almost had to fight them off, as they tried to climb into the trucks. For five days we collected and returned eighty tradesmen, who did a fabulous job of restoring the building and preparing it for the grand opening on Friday night, 28 September, 1945, by Major-General Foster, DSO, CBE, GOC, Fourth Canadian, ARMD Division.

Half way through, the contractor came to me with tears in his eyes, lamenting his treatment. He said, "You are employing free labour. How can I make any percentage?" I went to the Town Major with my problem. He suggested that an arrangement be made with the Commandant to pay the labour, and that this money go into the Camp funds. We would then pay a commission on this amount to Seppen. I demurred and said that we would all have to pay for this on our income tax when we got home. His instructions prevailed, however.

The big "shocker" though, was still to come – a bill from the architect for 1100 Guilders! I treated it as a joke and discarded it. Subsequently he visited me and, when I quizzed the item "For services rendered", he told me that he had obtained the contractor for us. I was dumbfounded and blurted, "Hell will freeze over before we will pay that bill." He completely wiped me out when he said, as he was about to leave, "At least the Germans paid their bills." I retorted, "I have just come back from Berlin and there is lots and lots of work for you in that city."

Again I went to the Town Major. He heard my story and answered, "Murray, we will have to pay it." Again I fought it, but it was futile. He went on, "Our government has instructed us to pay all bills regardless of their ridiculousness. You should see some of the claims we receive for garden furniture use and repair – sometimes triple the cost of actual replacement." So again I went down swinging!

When Major-General Foster opened the Maple Leaf Club on September 28, we had many local dignitaries in attendance. Prior to the opening, there was a big job in the selection of staff. I hired a fine hotel manager, Henri de Graff, and we set out to procure the best club staff in northwest Europe. An advertisement in the local newspaper brought hundreds of applicants. Upon arriving at the 10 a.m. appointed time, the line of applicants was two blocks long. Henri and I found it impossible to fight our way through the front door, what with the crush of aspirants and the impeding bicycles. We often laughed later about how we eventually had to settle by entering through a basement window.

We soon discovered that 95% of the girls wished to be receptionists, but we only needed four for that job. No one wanted to be a waitress; seemingly, in Holland, being a waitress carried a demeaning connotation. So, if we were keenly interested in the applicant, we invariably had to visit her parents to obtain permission. Before we did all this, however, we first cleared all our "possibles" with the local police authorities.

Most of the employees we hired had little in the way of attire, so, on a trip to an Amsterdam textile plant one day, we uncovered just a sufficient number of floral frocks to give two to each member of staff. The troops often commented on how nattily attired everyone was. Our complement numbered 111 civilians and 10 military personnel.

We were open from 7 a.m. to 10 p.m. daily on a two-shift basis. Besides restaurant facilities, we offered many other services, including clothes pressing, barbershop, games, writing and mailing rooms – also a pleasant chapel furnished with solid oak pews and chairs. We also "liberated" an old German bus, overhauled it, and ran conducted tours to Paris, Brussels, and one to Berlin.

On our staff we had a talented cartoonist, Jan Nieuwenhuys. Several of his painted works adorned our club, bringing much praise from the guests. He was particularly adept at portraying a Canadian soldier as seen through the eyes of a Dutchman. We also had Canadian cartoonists, notably Bing Coughlin, who skilfully captured our troops as seen through Canadian eyes.

I felt that something should be done towards putting Jan's best into book form. In Amsterdam I contacted De La Mar, one of Holland's biggest prewar lithographers, taking in the posters and discussing a possible publication as a souvenir for the departing Canucks. They assured me that it could be done, and the total cost for the four-colour job would be 30 000 Guilders, or 3 Guilders each. After some consideration, and receiving a promise of fast delivery, I gave the order.

Every time I was in Amsterdam I would drop in to view the progress and, more often, to cajole them. They were dastardly slow on the plate work. Then one morning I was shocked to read the headline of the daily *Maple Leaf* which said in large bold letters – Canadians get the 'Lizzie'. The item went on to say that the *Queen Elizabeth* could hoist a whole division on a single trip. I was sick, but

Chalkboard activity signs at the Maple Leaf Club

The YMCA touring vehicle, a "liberated" German bus

Cover of the booklet Daag, *a collection of cartoons about Canadian troop activities in the Netherlands*

Newspaper headline of Special Victory Edition of The Maple Leaf

managed to drive to De La Mar to show them the *Maple Leaf* copy. They promised to get cracking. About every second day, I was on their threshold, but now I was resorting to bribery and plied the artisans with cigarettes.

Then, about four weeks later, another startling announcement in *Maple Leaf* – "The last division, Division 4, will be exiting Holland on Saturday 8 December 1945."

Again I took the edition into De La Mar management, scolding them for not keeping their promise. I warned them that if the order was not complete by the night of December 7th, I would disclaim all responsibility and it would be their job to peddle them to the Dutch populace. Good luck! I knew, and they knew, that no canny Dutchman would pay the equivalent of almost three bucks to be reminded of Canadians. I, too, was experiencing some bad dreams, thinking of the horrible possibility of being incarcerated in the Netherlands until I peddled my way through 10 000 copies of *Daag*.

On the afternoon of 7 December 1945, we dispatched a sixty-hundred-weight to De La Mar, loaded the consignment and headed for Ostend. The following morning we nailed the Fourth Division lads as they boarded the train on their first leg homeward-bound. It was an "easy sell" and they grabbed them – a fine souvenir to take away. I returned to Amsterdam with the artist and the money. I will never forget the laying down of 30 000 Guilders on the president's big desk, and the profound sense of relief that came over me as I did it. He turned over 3000 Guilders to Jan, and then presented a be-ribboned and autographed copy of *Daag* to me. Every time I stumble upon it in a file, it brings back a host of memories.

The Maple Leaf Club was selected as the one club to remain open for Christmas, in order to take care of the tag ends of the troops still remaining in northwest Europe. We put on a lavish party on Christmas Day and followed up with an equally fine farewell "bash" for the staff on the 26th. I spent many hours preparing a speech in Dutch for the occasion. It was supposed to be serious, but it provoked rounds of laughter, so I assumed that my Dutch was not perfect.

Before leaving the Maple Leaf Club saga, I would like to make mention of a huge sign, illuminated by spotlights and erected on the peak of the building. Cut-out letters, four feet in height, faced in tinfoil, spelled out "Merry Christmas." It could be seen from any point in the city. Later, I was to learn that a local minister had used this sign as the theme for his Christmas sermon, claiming that it was a farewell from their liberators.

I boarded the old *Aquitania* at Liverpool on January 28th for what turned out to be a turbulent trip back to Canada. The old sea captain was to tell us that it was his roughest passage in twenty-eight years. I still recall pacing the deck and seeing that venerable ship almost pulling apart under my feet.

When having a haircut one day, I noticed a toy koala bear for sale in the barbershop. They were asking $20, and it seemed a lot. I thought of it for Dave and, although they reminded me it was their only one, I said that the size of the expenditure deserved careful consideration. However, a day later, I returned and discovered it still on display, so I splurged and bought it. When David met me later in Hamilton, he grabbed it, and over a span of several years, he loved "Koala" to the point of obscenity!

Arriving back at The Horse Palace in Toronto on February 7th, we were all required to go through a thorough medical. Of course, it ground to a halt again; it seemed that every MO wanted to have a listen to my heart. I finally lost my patience and announced, "My heart is no different than it was at the time of induction and, while I appreciate my government's interest in me, I do not want to involve certain medics in my case. Please give me that release form, that I may sign it and join the group heading for Hamilton and home."

Outdoor sign for The Maple Leaf Club

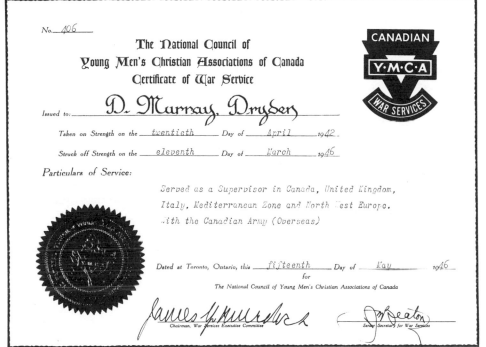

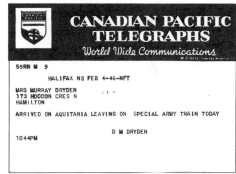

A telegram from Halifax, Nova Scotia announcing Murray's return in 1946

YMCA Certificate of War Service

Murray's officer's cap

CHAPTER SIX

Postwar Years

Aquella business representative card

Upon arrival home from overseas in 1946, I had been anxious to get back into sales work. An article in the current edition of *Reader's Digest* and *Forbes Business Magazine* entitled "Water Stay Away From My Wall" grabbed my attention. It concerned the Maginot Line in France, and how its designers had come up with red faces when they discovered the fortification was too damp to accommodate troops or for storing of munitions. A new discovery – an award-winning material called "Aquella" – supposedly made it habitable, if not impregnable.

When these articles hit the newsstand, all hell broke loose! Letters by the thousands flooded in, inquiring about this wonder product. A large segment of the populace wanted to remedy that universal problem – wet basements. The New York office was stormed by people seeking the franchise for Aquella.

One businessman from Alabama arrived with a briefcase full of credentials and he was Mr. Alabama himself. Within a few minutes, the sales manager had turned over full franchise rights for the state and, in return, received an order for thirteen carloads. As the customer headed for the door, the manager's conscience bothered him at taking such an easy order. He stopped his client, saying, "I know how good Aquella is, but I want to make sure that *you* know how good it is so that you can sell it to someone else." The gentleman from Alabama dismissed it all with a wave of the hand, saying "I'se don't care if it's hoss shit – so long as it sells, it's good!" (Is this typical North American merchandising philosophy as we know it?)

It was too late when I got to New York, but I did get the name of the Ontario distributors and decided to contact them. The firm, Construction Supplies Ltd. engaged me to cover the province, appointing dealers and agents. Again, I wanted to work on a straight commission basis. The parent company, Prima Products of New York, sent their sales manager up to Ontario to go around the territory with me.

My big problem was in getting a car. In those early post-war days, they were just not available. Where to get one? – of everyone I met, I asked the question. One afternoon, in Hamilton, I ran into a friend and I inquired of him. He replied that he had just come through Welland about two hours before and had noticed a car in Mason and Kells' window. However, when he told me that it was a Hudson, I replied, "Thanks, but that is too rich for me." However, I went home and talked it over with Margaret. We decided to phone the dealer and tell him to hold it for us and that we would be down that evening to take possession.

It turned out that the vehicle had no bumpers, no horn, no chrome stripping – and no back seat! However, it did have wheels. We were promised the rest of the car when the items became available. The cheque we gave in payment completely scuppered our bank account. (We always felt guilty driving that big car, and over 100 000 miles later, both of us were relieved when we got our first of what became a long series of 6-cylinder Fords.)

I will never forget the first morning I drove out on the territory with the Hudson. After filling its gas tank, my financial resources were zilch. My first call that Monday morning was on a hardware store in Bowmanville, where I got a nice order. In 1971, I returned to Mr. McGregor to tell him just how much that order had meant to me that day.

Over a period of three years, I set up 240 Aquella dealers across the province, my travel averaging almost 35 000 miles each year. While the product was good, the price was too high to attain any kind of volume. I wanted to acquire other related lines to help cover some of my expenses, but my firm wanted to have jurisdiction, and kept saying that they would procure other product lines. It never happened, and the road expenses continued to eat me up.

With a small financial boost from my parents, I then decided to publish a travel book, as I knew Ontario "like the back of my hand". Instead of getting into games at night, I used my evenings gathering reliable travel information on Ontario. This guide covered recommended eating and sleeping accommodations, entertainment, sightseeing, service clubs, automobile dealers and highway information. It gave only the thumbnail details, along with prices and rates. No advertising was sold, making sure that all the information was unprejudiced.

Murray's family at the 1947 reunion: back row *Robert, Jean, Murray, Amy, Andrew;* front row *Edna, father, mother, Helen*

A 1947 get-together of Murray's brothers and other relatives returned from war service

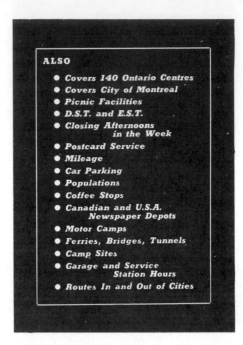

Cover of Ontario Guest Service guide

ALSO

- Covers 140 Ontario Centres
- Covers City of Montreal
- Picnic Facilities
- D.S.T. and E.S.T.
- Closing Afternoons in the Week
- Postcard Service
- Mileage
- Car Parking
- Populations
- Coffee Stops
- Canadian and U.S.A. Newspaper Depots
- Motor Camps
- Ferries, Bridges, Tunnels
- Camp Sites
- Garage and Service Station Hours
- Routes In and Out of Cities

ONTARIO GUEST SERVICE

1948-49
Accurate Information
$1.00

Highway Routes   Tourist Inquiry
Coming Events   Service Clubs
Entertainment   Sightseeing

RECOMMENDED EATING AND
SLEEPING ACCOMMODATIONS

We called the travel guide the *Ontario Guest Service* and printed 6000 copies each year for the four editions. It was a massive job, and here Margaret did yeoman service. One of the hardest things we encountered was turning the regular purchasers off after we ceased publication.

While we did not make money commensurate with the effort, the guide did serve a very real need in the lives of both of us. Considering that my commission earnings were running a mere $3000 a year, there is no doubt in my mind that I would have given up long before the three years, had I not thought that the publication would supplement our income once it became better known to the travelling public. Looking back now, *Ontario Guest Service* played an important part, in a defensive way, by providing a sort of delaying action until we hooked into what later became such a successful brick-and-block venture.

KIWANIS

For years, I had wanted to be a member of a service club; however, my constant travelling of Ontario highways made it impractical, as I could never meet the guidelines for service. Then, when we moved from Hamilton to Toronto, where I was able to confine my economic pursuits to the metropolitan area, I was eager to join the Kiwanis Club.

One day, calling on customer Charlie Leachman, who was sporting the "K" pin, I summoned up sufficient courage to make an inquiry. He told me that he was a member of the West Toronto Casa Loma Club but that I resided in the Kingsway Club area. He promised to have one of that club's members, Norman Irwin – an architect, contact me. Later, when discussing the detailed application

74

form, we ran into a classification roadblock. He told me that there were only executives in Kiwanis. I replied that I had just begun working with my present company and that I was a mere salesman. My interviewer finally decided to categorize me as "Sales Representative – Building Materials".

I was subsequently accepted by the Board and, on 17 November 1949, was inducted into the Kiwanis Club of the Kingsway. Immediately following the meeting and congratulatory handshakes, Dr. Everett Leyland, in charge of programme, asked me to thank the speaker at the next week's luncheon.

I declined, saying I had never done it before, but that I planned on taking a public speaking course that winter, and to see me in the spring. However, he was adamant, reminding me that I had joined Kiwanis to do a job, and he refused to accept "No" for an answer. I came perilously close to resigning on the spot and entering the *Guiness Book of Records* for shortest membership.

To make matters worse, my father was visiting us and I had already issued him an invitation to the luncheon. I fretted and worried all week, and no speaker in our club, either before or since, has ever been so poorly thanked. I put on a pathetic performance in front of my father. I guess that I did improve, however, as I went on to become President in 1957 and Lieutenant-Governor of our division in 1959.

I was determined to make sacrifices in my presidential year and, at times, I sensed some of the membership balking as I drove them to new heights. We chartered the first Brampton club, followed by the Humber Valley Club. Our membership soared. I soon learned, though, that a volunteer brigade can be pushed only so far. It was not an infrequent occurrence to have a committee chairman let me down. I found it difficult to shake off an almost-persecution complex. (In fact, I understand perfectly what our son Ken is saying on page 239 of his book *The Game.* ". . . Those who didn't backcheck as often as I thought

Murray and Margaret, the couple on the right, during a Kiwanis convention at the Chateau Laurier, Ottawa, 1957

they should, those who drank too much, let *me* down. They had seemed more like opponents than teammates, lined up against me, ...")

Our club, for the first time in its 37-year history, won the Henry Elliot Memorial Gong, highest achievement award for the Eastern Canada District, as well as winning Honourable Mention at the international level.

The Kiwanis organization has been good for me and to me. Dozens of clubs, including Rotary and Lions across the world, now support Sleeping Children Around the World.

I heartily endorse a service club experience for anyone desirous of making a contribution to his or her community.

In 1950, I was approached by the Etobicoke YMCA-YWCA and asked to serve on the Board of Directors. It was a happy association over a period of sixteen years, during which I served as President for two years (1963, 1964).

Dave with his Grandfather Dryden

TAX PROBLEMS

It was near the end of the 1948-49-50 period that I ran into problems with the Receiver-General. The National Revenue office in Hamilton seriously questioned my claim for travelling expenses. I claimed that I had travelled 30 000 miles a year for each of three years. I had carelessly kept incomplete records of all my road expenses. In those days, it did not seem so important. The much-publicized rule was that you could charge 75% of your mileage to business at six cents a mile, with the remaining 25% a personal responsibility.

Mr. Kershaw, an inspector, contended that I could not have done the volume of business I had if I travelled that many miles. Too, his office found it hard to understand that I would work for three full years, continuing to mire myself financially. They possibly could have accepted one year and, logically, they were right. But, in view of three years' hard work, long hours, and financial torture, these sessions with the National Revenue people drove me almost to the brink. I began to feel sorry for myself, and this was dangerous.

Three years of worry, using up our savings and wartime service establishment credits, going into debt, and then to be assessed extra income tax, was difficult to accept. However, just when everything seemed lost, the senior inspector, Mr. Ray Madden, called me for an interview. After we had finished, he said, "I believe you." What a relief that decision was!

Before I left his office that day, he offered me a position in his department. Needless to say, I was overwhelmed but, without appearing unappreciative, I told him that my limited academic training would prejudice my going very far in the Civil Service. I sincerely thanked him for his display of confidence under the circumstances, and hoped that he would understand my position. Mired in debt, I had to stick to sales, the only field I knew.

Years later, I kept saying to myself, "I must go in and see Mr. Madden." It wasn't until just before my retirement that I found myself again in Hamilton and on Main Street, where Internal Revenue had moved its offices some years before from the Post Office. While I was on a tight schedule that particular day, I made the time and was always glad afterwards that I had. I was quite surprised that Mr. Madden was still with the department, although on the verge of retirement.

I told him why I had come back, and how much his decision, back in 1948, had influenced my life. I recounted our dialogue of some twenty years before, my precarious and confused mental state at the time, and how easy it would have been for him to tip me over into becoming an out-and-out radical. I told him that maybe relating my experience could help some other person in the future. I also said that his judgement had paid off for his employer who, in the meantime, had done pretty well in getting even, now that I was in a position to pay substantial income tax! Upon parting, he thanked me profusely for coming back, volunteering that I was the first one who had. It was a good moment. . . .

HIGH FINANCE

Along with my entrepreneur adventures, there were some forays in other directions as well.

On a Saturday afternoon, in the winter of 1952, I was driving down Brown's Line when I spotted one of my construction business customers, Joe Bartman, going into his house. When I gave him the "toot", he signalled me to stop. He got into the car, and, in the course of our conversation, I mentioned that I had noticed in *McLean Reports* that he was going to construct a couple of houses.

He replied, "To heck with building, there is more money in uranium." Well, he got me so excited at the prospect of getting in on a "killing" that I could hardly wait to meet him at Davidson & Co. on Monday at ten. When the market opened, Gunnar took off and was too rich for my blood. However, the experts told me that Chimo was an adjoining property and that possibly I should consider it. A real "babe in the woods", this being my first gambling antic, I was almost on the verge of panic. I finally elected to purchase 1000 shares of Chimo at $3.30 a share, for which I was required to pay one half down with the order.

Worthless shares of Biltmore Hat Company

After the transaction had reached the point of no return, I suddenly thought about the matter of correspondence. I told Joe that there was no way I could allow the mail to come to my home. We were negotiating the building of a new house at the time and would need every cent for that. Of course, I was thinking that the investment venture might make it possible to add another room or two to our plans. Joe said, "No problem, we will have all mail come to my house."

Well, it was just like the "kiss of death". My stock commenced to toboggan the next day, and kept going down and down to the level where the margin was in jeopardy. Finally, I had to whack up more money. The situation deteriorated to the point where it seemed that I was driving over early to the house of our broker, Jack Dennis, about once a week and slipping another cheque through the letter slot. When the stock dipped down to 60¢ I paid the balance and then tried to forget it.

Another day, I got talking with my butcher and he claimed to have a hot tip. This one was on Arcan, and it supposedly had great potential. I sold the chips, took the $600, and plunged the whole amount into 300 shares of Arcan. Would you believe it? Within a year the company was bankrupt! All I have to show for my $3300 investment is the worthless Arcan stock certificate in my safety deposit box.

One night, several years later, when the whole family (now matured) was at the dinner table, I decided to regale them with the above story. It made me feel better to get the deceit off my chest, and I hoped the children would learn something from my escapades in high finance.

BILTMORE INDUSTRIES DEBACLE
More recently I had visions of men going back to wearing hats and had invested substantially in Biltmore Industries. While the hat industry had been subjected to several shocks (long hair styles, the Catholic Church no longer decreeing that women wear hats in church, the high coiffures, even the low-slung car door openings, etc.), this company had successfully diversified and had made a deal for Stetson to purchase the company with a conditional closing dateline.

Well, FIRA kicked it around until the deadline passed. Biltmore became involved in the western hat craze — to the point that they put on a night shift in order to cope with their orders (many from the USA). All of a sudden, these orders started to back up and the cancellations left them holding several million dollars in inventory.

In 1981, the Canadian Imperial Bank of Commerce forced the company into receivership. Stetson then came in and bought up the pieces, all of which went to CIBC. The common shareholders did not receive a penny – no, not even an explanation. They had to glean the sad story from the newspapers.

It was a devastating blow to Margaret and me. We were thankful for the Sleeping Children Around The World programme at the time, as we were so concerned for this project that it meant we could not dwell on the Biltmore calamity. In this sense, SCAW proved to be good therapy and we were determined that this setback in our lives was not going to affect the destiny of the project.

CHAPTER SEVEN

The Construction Business

There was rarely a dull moment during my twenty-four years engaged in the construction material business, I would like to relate just a few of the many humorous and not-so-humorous incidents that happened during those years.

Anyone who lived in Metropolitan Toronto immediately following the war will remember how that city literally exploded. A whole new crop of builders and would-be builders sprang up. So many did not know a block from a brick, and it is little wonder some of the houses built during that "boom" period left a lot to be desired.

One evening, in the Fall of 1949, while driving along Bogert Avenue in Willowdale, I spotted an excavator pulling out a long line of basements, so I stopped and chatted with the builder. When he told me that he would be needing, among other items, 5" concrete blocks, I knew right away that he was a "freshman". He expressed surprise that there was no such thing as a 5" block, but added that he had just come out of the "needle trade"!

During the war, several families with limited funds were able to get permits to construct basements only. Even concrete blocks were difficult to come by in those days. Many of these "rheumatic dugouts" were fitted up quite comfortably, so much so that the townships experienced real problems in pressuring the owners to complete their houses.

The first winter, I spent a great deal of my time canvassing these streets, principally in the northern section of Toronto. Streets like Cooper, Bedford Park, Woburn, and many others were largely occupied by these "cave dwellers". Often I had to stickhandle my way around a stack of empty beer cases and a cache of wine bottles before finding the trap-door entrance, which was usually level with the ground. Many of my calls were made at night so as to be able to talk to the husband. I would offer them cinder blocks that could later be covered with stucco, or a limited variety of bricks. It was invariably a tough sale, as most of the occupants were quite content in their cosy dugouts. However, the building departments of the municipalities kept "hammering" them, so that by the end of 1950 most of these "cellar dwellers" were experiencing "daylight" living. Many purchased the necessary materials and then hired the required tradesmen.

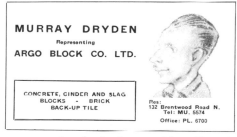

MURRAY DRYDEN
Representing
ARGO BLOCK CO. LTD.

CONCRETE, CINDER AND SLAG
BLOCKS - BRICK
BACK-UP TILE

Res:
132 Brentwood Road N.
Tel: MU. 5574
Office: PL. 6700

Another business card from Murray's collection

1953 catalogue for Murray's Building Supply Company

In order to blanket the Metropolitan Toronto area, so that our customers could reach us without long distance, we had Atwater, Murray, and Cedar exchanges coming into the office in our home. Then, to further improve our service, I had a telephone installed in the car.

Margaret handled all incoming calls during the day. She sure was a busy gal, customers often preferring to deal with her rather than me. Some of the ordering in those days was pathetic. Margaret had to contend with some "beauts" over the telephone. She still remembers a lady from North York calling and requesting a load of block. When quizzed as to whether it was concrete or cinder, she replied, "Just send whatever you have got!"

Every call was recorded with the time and what was said. Often, months later, controversial transactions were settled on information in these records. Using a standard wire-bound type of book over the twenty-four years, we built up an inventory of several hundred, and we still have them in our archives.

As our name had twelve letters, we used two clock faces as our trademark on all advertising – with a connecting painted strip with the words "7 a.m. to 10 p.m. service."

During construction months, it was not unusual to log 80 to 100 hours a week.

During the twenty-four-year span in which I was engaged as a manufacturer's agent in the masonry material business, I religiously set aside one night every two weeks for collections. Over that period I averaged a bit better than one million dollars' worth of sales per year. Sales are unimportant if you don't get paid for them.

I tried to select a night when Margaret would be going out. Following dinner and shower, and in my PJ's, I would take my ugly pills, place the two phones in bed along with my five "sweat sheets" and then hammer the delinquents from 7 to 10 p.m. Excuses ran the full gamut, and when the time came to put the telephones to bed, I was usually climbing the walls. However, this twice-monthly exercise proved a great teacher to me.

Ashamedly now, I admit that I possessed a few prejudices about certain races. I was to discover that there is only one yardstick by which to judge someone, and that is: Is that person honest or dishonest? I soon learned that no nationality has a corner on honesty. How I wish that everyone could have had my experience in dealing with the "melting pot" of the world. If so, I guarantee racial prejudice would be wiped out.

Frequently, when a customer would reach me at seven in the morning, he would try me next time at a quarter to seven, and then maybe at six-thirty. The same pattern developed at night, cutting further into the sleep period. However, in those days, quality and price were usually matched by your competitor, so it all boiled down to the one giving the better service getting the order.

The Dryden clocks advertising

Back in the late '40s and early '50s, some construction materials were often in short supply. Weeping tile was one such example, but transport was frequently an even greater problem. A manufacturer in St. Catharines would supply me with tile, provided I took delivery at night. It was the only time he could get a truck.

About twice a week, I would meet the truck driver at 9 p.m. at the old Six Points Hotel in Islington, where he would tarry long enough to slake his thirst. Then we would head out to a subdivision, armed with a powerful flashlight, and grope our way around as we unloaded 2500 tiles on as many as five different builders' job sites.

For several years, burnt clay and shale bricks were often impossible to obtain. Some disreputable manufacturers and agents refused to supply these scarce items unless they got the order for the basement blocks as well. As blocks came before bricks, frequently the builder, after putting in all his basements and having them backfilled, would wait fruitlessly for weeks before finally ending up ordering inferior, but available, concrete brick. As a matter of fact, burnt brick was such a scarce commodity that its manufacturers would refuse to deliver unless there was sufficient help on the site to hand-unload. This created friction between the supplier and the customer.

Sometimes we would run out of brick in the middle of building a house, and then face the problem of the next kiln load not matching. This happened to me one time after an Oakville customer had only half of the brickwork on a house completed. When we eventually delivered the last truckload, it happened to be raining and the wet red brick matched the previous brick perfectly. However, when the roof was on and the brickwork dried out, we had a glaring ensemble!

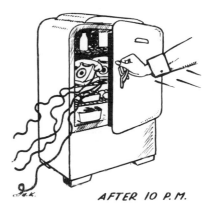

Murray's idea of how to keep the phones quiet

Murray with stockpile of bricks and 1955 Ford, from personalized postcard

Daughter Judy at 20 months; another use for an Argo block

The poor builder was at his wit's end. When the NHA inspector came in, to pass the all-important roof mortgage draw, my nervous customer pantomimed, "Me, I don't say *nothing*!"

One of the companies I represented owned a stone quarry at Glen Williams. Here they quarried Credit Valley random flagstone, later guillotining it to a width of four inches and selling it as Ledge Rock for facing on houses and commercial buildings. Because it was so irregular, bricklayers balked at laying it. Builders had to coerce them to lay a mere "bay" of it. I recall one incident in Bayview Village where the "brickies" could only be coaxed by a couple of cases of beer on the job. Well, the workmen started off well at ground level, but got progressively worse, graduating into a jumble by the time they reached the window-sill terminus!

One evening, I got a telephone call from a man who was building his own house on Pharmacy Avenue in Scarborough. He wanted to order Roman Brick. When I inquired, "What colour?" he replied, "I want all of them!" "But, there are six colours," I hastened to advise him. Unfazed, he said, "I know it, but I still want them all." It was quite a task figuring out the proper quantities to ship, because there were three different sizes (regular, roman, and header) in each colour. If you think my job was hard, it was nothing compared to that of the bricklayers. When I visited the site on a couple of occasions, the "brickies" were going "bananas". Dazzled by a choice of eighteen different bricks, it necessitated lengthy study before each brick was laid. The finished product, still standing, resembles "Jacob's coat".

And I like the story of the house on Faith Avenue in North York. Its owner had lived in the basement for several years, then managed to go up with cinder blocks and to get a roof on the structure. He plastered three sides and then undertook to simulate Permastone on its front – Queen Anne fronts and Betty Anne backs, as we called them. An attempt was made to form the cement plaster into stone shapes. Then, I swear, every night he must have gone out with paint of a different color, daubing these stones with seven colours, including yellow, red, and green. Needless to say, it was hideous. One of my customers, Saunders Construction, several years later built a few houses across the road, and poor Max had a terrible time selling them. Prospects would look out of the living-room picture window and flee! Much later, he did sell them (after dark).

It never ceased to amaze me how many builders would attempt to cut corners on the exteriors of their houses. I constantly reminded them that, while purchasers could later alter or replace anything concerning the interior, the "skin" of a house remained fixed.

A developer, Ken Bunston, driving into his Valecrest subdivision one day, felt that a house being built near the entrance by Johnson & McFadden was not on the correct lot. A subsequent inspection of the plan for the subdivision disclosed that the already roofed house was indeed halfway over on another contractor's property. For the new, inexperienced and modestly financed builders, there were no options. The misplaced structure had to be torn down, even if it meant financial ruin. When the six other builders involved on the inner circle heard of the calamitous mistake, they called a meeting with the developer and offered to give up a foot here, a few inches there, from their lots, enabling the errant house to remain where it stood. It was the finest display of practical Christianity – an act that gave a lot of people a nice warm feeling.

One of my customers built a 79-house subdivision in North Toronto. I approached him about burnt clay brick, but he said that until he knew his costs, he would have to use run-of-the-mill trades and go with the cheapest quality concrete bricks.

After he had completed the first half-dozen units, I went back to see him. When he admitted that his profit was almost unconscionable, I asked whether he would be going ahead with burnt clay brick on the remainder. His reply: "Why should I when I have umpteen houses sold ahead of the excavator?" Long after the subdivision was completed, one of the buyers got hold of an architectural plan and noted that the builder had arbitrarily substituted an open arch for a door. He organized the other owners, and the mortgage company forced the builder to come back and install the missing seventy-nine doors.

Another "short pants" builder got off on the wrong foot in Islington around 1949 by bringing in the shovel and excavating on the Sabbath. Later, this same housebuilder was having difficulty with some of his customers. He claimed that they were going into his construction shack at night and stealing some of the better quality lumber. In an effort to scare off the culprits, he painted skull and crossbones on the long side of the building with the wording "Leave that wood alone or die!" When this did not stop them, he rigged a contraption involving a can of white paint over the top of the door. Yes, you guessed it! After waiting several days to trap the marauders, one morning – hurriedly and unthinkingly – he became the victim of his own invention!

Murray in his typically marked car, beside a stockpile of concrete blocks

A painting contractor, Albert Chiarandini, who built several houses in the 1950s and now, some 30 years later, instructs a class in landscape painting, also encountered problems with pilferers and appealed to them in a different way. He had neat signs made to place on the inside of the living room windows of his houses carrying the inscription GOD DOES NOT MAKE THIEVES. This same builder was a cunning psychologist. He erected signs after his houses were fully completed that read NOT FOR SALE YET. He had pleading prospects galore!

It was not unknown for builders to employ small acts of bribery to get a load of material quickly. I often related some of these humorous incidents to my family. One night, dining at the home of teetotal friends in North Toronto, our Ken, who was seven at the time, was regaling our hosts at the table with a lengthy and impossible dissertation. It went on and on, and just when I was wondering how he was going to bring it all to some sort of logical conclusion, he suddenly climaxed, ". . . and I give you a bottle of whisky!" I tell you, it was a howler, and these friends still enjoy kidding us.

As I travel around this great city, its houses continue to remind me of episodes connected with them.

I am sure that you have often wondered how some streets got their names. A goodly number can be traced back to the subdivider. Some of the names are downright amusing, often bordering on the ridiculous – e.g., Rabbit Lane, Radio Valve Road. . . . Contractors and subdividers naturally tried to get a street named after themselves. If the name was already in use, then they would concoct a name – e.g., partners Carl and Nathan came up with Carnat Road.

One of my customers, building a group of houses on a keyhole street, newly named Winesap Place, blamed its alcoholic connotation for the reluctance of buyers. He had made overtures to Etobicoke Township to have the name moved out to Applewood Acres, a more suitable environment, when suddenly the houses commenced to sell! He told me later that attitudes had changed when real estate and prospective buyers began pronouncing it "Win-sap".

At my retirement dinner in 1972, I confessed failure in not getting a street named after me in Metropolitan Toronto. I had suggested "Dryden Drive" (I like rhythmic names) to several subdividers, but now I was prepared to settle for "Dryden Alley".

Looking back, it is hard to believe all that was accomplished in those years. Hats have to be doffed to the immigrants who flooded into Canada immediately following the war. They made a great contribution to many communities and to this country. And how these New Canadians worked, and in most cases without the benefit of any type of union!

Most tradesmen were employed on a piecework basis. I smile, thinking back on some of the incidents . . . Checking a job in Port Credit, the masonry contractor asked me to ship in a load of concrete blocks. As I was driving away to seek a telephone, he shouted, "Tell them if they can't ship the blocks to send a deck of cards!" Then there was the masonry contractor who usually had three or four apartment jobs going on at one time. He would start one gang at 7 a.m. and set a furious pace for his bricklayers to follow. When they had developed a full head of steam, so to speak, he would rush off to another job and "set a fire" under the group there. He did this all day and it was surprising how long the momentum carried on after he had left each job.

Concrete and drain contractors were the hardest workers and put in the longest hours in the construction industry. I had an Italian customer, Frank Ciaschini, who fitted perfectly into this category. About three times a year, my phone would ring just after 6 a.m. On one of these occasions, I staggered to the impatient intruder, lifted the receiver, and, in my best groggy voice, said, "Good morning, Frank." After about five seconds' silence, I heard, "How the hell did you know it was Frank?" I replied, "You are the only sonofagun who gets me out of bed at 6.15 a.m." Laughingly, he instructed, "Send me a coupla tous weeps" (2000 weeping tile).

At least one builder was not satisfied with confining himself to a daylight programme. Rex Hislop not only planned a 24-hour-a-day operation, he did it in all seasons. Hislop pioneered Toronto's Rexdale area. It was quite a sight to follow the feverish activity in his subdivision. Huge tarpaulin tents were erected over each single excavation so that tradesmen, with the benefit of lights and oil heaters, were able to work around the clock.

Then there were the two young lads operating under the contracting title Amos & Carson. Boy, how those guys could lay heavy 10" and 12" concrete blocks. One time I quizzed them as to how many they could lay in a day. The answer: "About 800 – but at night I tell you we go home and leave our wives alone!"

The "designated shippers" had a rough time in the heavy masonry business. Customers constantly called and "conned" the transport department. To hear them tell it, every job was paved to the hole. For the better part of ten postwar years, most building permits were issued before the essential services were put in place. Trucks, laden with concrete basement block, often were required to cross perilous fields. Springtime was murder. Vehicles would become hopelessly

Ken and Dave roasting their father at his retirement dinner, 1972

Murray being awakened at seven in the morning

mired, requiring the help of bulldozers, but not always successfully. Even those bulldozers got bogged down, necessitating the calling in of a larger one to winch them out. One of my firms still claims it lost one of its trucks *entirely* in the Glen Agar subdivision!

This subdivision created so much "flak" for the Etobicoke Council that they eventually passed a by-law prohibiting the issuing of building permits until all essential services were in place. The councillors had become fed up with contingents of the new rubber-booted homeowners storming weekly meetings of Council.

My first call one morning was on Hartib Construction in Islington. I arrived just as Harry Woods, the builder, was emerging from a house that had just been occupied the night before. The harassed contractor was holding three sheets of paper that had just been handed to him by the new owner. These sheets listed 73 complaints about the house. My distraught customer read off a number of the "beefs" (many of a ridiculous nature) and then remarked, "I don't know whether to tear down the house and start over again, or to slip around the corner to the Islington House and get drunk!"

One of my customers, who was building in North Toronto, "staked" out three residences on what before had been a baseball diamond. When the excavator came in, he discovered that all the stakes had been pulled out. Again, the builder laid out the basements, but this time he cut out small squares of sods around the stakes. Undaunted, the baseballers returned, performing an absolute miracle with neat-fitting replacement sod. The third stake-out called for round-the-clock services of an on-site guard until the excavator arrived!

Alas, I could never say enough about my customers, many of whom began in the construction business at the same time I did. Fellow salesmen often scoffed and referred to me as "One-house Dryden". I reminded them that they would grow, and they did grow too – and I with them! Many of them went on to become the leading housebuilders in Metropolitan Toronto. While a handful did find their way into the opposition camp, the vast bulk did remain loyal. Indeed, over the years, quite a few of them became good friends of mine.

Bill Pronk – a genial, gangling, raw-boned Hollander – was one of my favourite customers, even if he did wield a sharp pencil. Frequently I would meet him around ten and go for a morning coffee. Most Dutchmen, I discovered, cannot face the day without that morning pick-me-up.

One day, Bill had just returned from his coffee break when I arrived. He was not in his usual carefree mood. Kidding him about his disposition, I inquired if he had happened to be on the receiving end of a bum cup of java. "Worse still," he replied, "do you know that coffee shop has raised its price from 5 cents to 10?" And he went on, "Well, I've got news for them! I can still get it for a nickel down at Woolworth's." Poor Bill (long deceased), I have often wondered since then how he would ever be able to navigate in the present 50¢-plus environment.

Returning from a trip to Japan in the early 1950s, I brought into Canada one of the first air polluters, the transistor pocket radio. Coming in from the airport that day, I distinctly remember the taxi driver becoming disturbed by sounds

The Dryden's breakfast hour. Murray used cartoons to enliven his catalogues

from an unidentified source. Snugly fitted into my shirt pocket was my radio, which I had flicked on as I entered his cab. For several weeks I had a barrel of fun with it on job sites driving customers mad, some of whom were scared that "dementation" had set in.

* * *

Shortly after moving from Hamilton to Toronto I had had a verbal commitment for a $1500 loan from the Manager, Jim Harding, at the Bank of Toronto at Royal York and Bloor. When I went in to sign the necessary documents, I discovered that Harding had been replaced by a Mr. Wilson. It just so happened that he had been transferred from the branch in North Toronto where my former employer, Concrete Products, did their banking.

Wilson would lend the money only on the condition that I would sign over my insurance policies. I fought this edict as Margaret was not well at the time (her blood count had reached a point where a crippling effect had set in). I feared this risk would devastate her. However, Mr. Wilson was adamant and I was desperate, so I had to level with Margaret and ask her to go down to the bank and sign the policies over. It was hard on both of us.

In the months ahead, our business began to prosper and it was not long before we were able to pay off the loan and reclaim the policies – a great relief to both of us, I can tell you.

* * *

On one occasion, I made an appointment to see Dick Grimm, Sales Manager of Argo Block Limited. I said to him, "Getting these size cheques from you is ridiculous." His reply was, "Forget it. Remember, the more money you make, the more I make. I hope you make twice as much next month."

Again, sometime during the early '60s, Bill Yeats, Sales Manager of Booth Brick, called me in to discuss remuneration. He told me, "We have been reviewing your position and feel that we should consider raising your commission."

I replied, "Forget it. You looked after me well during the sellers' market. Now maybe I can help you." I added, "Your volume is down, as is your price. How can you afford to increase your selling costs?" He replied, "All right, then, but we will review the matter in a year's time," to which I replied, "So far as I am concerned, you need never review it."

Well, a year later, almost to the day, Bill Yeats called me into his office and emphatically announced: "As of next month, your commission will be increased (almost double). It is on instructions of F.W. (Booth), *and* there is not a thing you can do about it." Little wonder that I found my work such a joy. . . .

There is one aspect that I must not neglect to mention. It concerns the loyalty of my employers and customers. Without this, we would never have been in a financial position to operate our Third World venture: *Sleeping Children Around the World*. At every opportunity, where our paths happen to cross, I remind them of just that. Their contributions to SCAW were immeasurable.

Time off with Margaret, Dave, and Ken, visiting parents in Winnipeg one Christmas holiday

THE INEVITABLE SPRING-FALL BRICK LIST.

Murray's supporting home staff

CHAPTER EIGHT

The Christmas Tree Business

When I look at my new coming-on-stream field of 30 000 Christmas trees, I think of them as a plantation of children's beds, as every three trees represent potential sleeping comfort for some bedless kiddie through our organization "Sleeping Children Around the World".

Margaret wondered why, in my forties, I had to choose Christmas Tree farming for a new challenge, with all its hazards and frustrations. I pointed out to her even more horrible examples of what some of our male friends had taken up during

Tree farm at Newmarket in midsummer

this period in their lives. Of course, when you reach the "Faithful Fifties" you wonder whatever possessed you to go off on the tangent.

Margaret was so anxious, at one time, that we just sell the properties and get free of all the perpetual every-season headaches . . . but I felt that the jury was still out.

Here is a copy of a letter I wrote to a friend back in 1971 on the subject of the Christmas Tree business:

Colorado blue spruce balled and bagged for move to transplanting site

"In the beginning, let me say that I wish I had never become involved! I purchased three properties in 1955 and I did not wish to be a parasite and merely sit on the land. I was anxious to make the property productive. Christmas trees at the time seemed to be a good crop. Unfortunately, a lot of other people thought the same way at the same time.

"While my experience was identical on all three properties, I will merely recount the details of activities on the larger farm.

"Unable to procure sufficient seedlings in Ontario, I had to import 100 000 two-year transplants from Zundert, Holland. I had them planted by the end of April, and we did not get any rain for six weeks.

"Each weekend I visited the farm and saw the extreme dryness wither the wee seedlings in the sandy soil. I ended up with 6000. I ordered another 100 000 for the next spring. That time I was luckier; I had a 90% catch. Since that time I have had to spray the field several times for the latest kind of infestation as Scotch Pine is afflicted with myriad diseases.

"The trade wants a dense tree, which means that you have to prune closely. After the third year, we had to begin pruning. This costs around five cents a tree. Labour is rough to procure, and of course there are all the various forms to fill out for the many government departments. Details of minimum wage, unemployment insurance, pension and workmen's compensation are only part of the paper work. Fighting the bugs, your bank manager, cajoling pruners in the heat of July, then coming home to the bookkeeping, sure take all the sex out of the business.

"We have had hail damage, two plagues of mice, losing 10% each year, another 10% to rabbits, plus ravages of the European Sawfly. We have also had two invasions of Pine Grosbeaks. These critters gobble the fresh buds on the leaders in early January and deform the tree. There is no way of combatting them. I also lost some 3000 trees when a neighbour decided to burn off some dead grass one spring. And, also there have been the tree thefts.

"All this means that it takes some seven years to grow a six-foot tree. A tree is pruned a minimum of five times (25¢ per tree) and you are indeed fortunate if you harvest one of every two planted.

"Then you must add property taxes, seedling and planting costs, plus costs of cutting and dragging the tree, to all your hard work, disappointments and frustrations.

"When offered a 90¢-on-the-stump price, I levelled with my bank manager and enlisted his help for a loan. At 90¢ a tree, I would have gone

Ballantrae farm under snow

Ken preparing a tree for its stand

Murray with bagged boughs — the locked-in aroma

bankrupt. I told him that my only hope was to use longer-handled pruning knives so as to prune the trees higher, holding them back from the market until prices became realistic. The bank went along with me. Prices improved each year, and in about five years, trees actually became scarce.

"During this shake-out period, we started a "choose-and-cut" operation for the public as a fund-raiser for Sleeping Children Around the World. Soon after that we got in the black, and have been ever since."

But that was not the end of our troubles. Late one night, back in 1979, I was served with a Supreme Court writ at our home. The plaintiff, a Norene Smith, was claiming one half of our Newmarket property, saying that her name had been forged on the deed. A lawyer working on another case had discovered the discrepancy and had encouraged the plaintiff to sue me.

When I had bought the property 24 years earlier from Mr. Armand Woodcock, he apparently had taken the son and the younger daughter (dressed up in high heels and adult clothes) and had the latter swear in front of an unknown Toronto lawyer that she was her sister, Norene. All three parties signed the deed. The father, the son, and the younger daughter had since died, as had my lawyer.

Even though I had paid the taxes for all those 24 years, and even though each party was responsible for his or her own legal costs, my legal advisers dissuaded me from fighting the case. I learned, too, that the witnessing lawyer had immunity from lawsuit, after six years, for witnessing a fraudulent signature. (That is not surprising when one considers that the governing body of Canada is top-heavy with lawyers.)

I had spent 80-90 hours a week on commission to buy that land, and it had meant many weekends and holidays planting, pruning and spraying. It almost seems that property does not belong to him that hath – but to him who hath the power to take it away. Our law appears to protect the forger. Never again will I accept a lawyer's affidavit on any important document!

In conversation with a Justice at Osgoode Hall, I pointed out that this member of the legal fraternity had taken an affidavit from a stranger off the street. While I reminded the learned gentleman how easily one could be wiped out by the forged stroke of a pen, he told me that there was no way to prevent this from happening. I replied that, to obtain a Canadian passport these days, they ask you for everything but a saliva test — surely an expensive property, more important than a passport, should have similar protection.

THE CHRISTMAS TREE DRAG

By a supporter of this special event.

It's quite a sight. . . the snow in the bush on a wintery, typical Canadian pre-Christmas Sunday. . . the children, full of expectation, romping with those lusty but loveable dogs from among the 40 or so sent by the St. Bernard Club of Ontario and the Newfoundland Dog Club of Canada.

Then out into the Ontario bush for that special Scotch Pine, with shouts of glee when the right one is found — cries of "Here's a great tree! Let's hitch it to this dog."

Guided back from the bush by the sound of Christmas carols coming from the trailer, the dogs proudly dragging the selected tree, the children find hot chocolate available and Santa waiting to have a word with them.

As the tree is paid for and the dogs' tips added to the Sleeping Children Around the World funds, there seems to be a link between that family. . . that child and the child in the Third World. If only they could join in this scene and the children could romp together!

The monetary rewards for our SCAW fund have been only part of the 30-year Christmas Tree story. Even with all the aggravation, there have been lots of pluses. Often I will prune in the cool of a summer evening until about 8 o'clock. I then roll out the foam-rubber mattress and eat my picnic supper while enjoying the beautiful sunset. It is so peaceful and quiet, almost like being in Algonquin Park.

The scent from nearly 40 000 pines, the full moon and the sound of the whip-poor-will quickly lull me into sleepland. I am usually awakened by the birds singing and the squirrels flitting over my head just as the sun rises around six, when I turn on the car radio and listen to the CFRB short devotional programme. Never have I felt closer to God. . . .

A family selecting and cutting "their" tree

Road lined with cars during the annual Christmas-tree drag at Caledon

Murray doing his summer pruning at the Caledon farm

CHAPTER NINE

Family and Sports

Murray and Margaret in 1938

Let me say a few words about our three children, and how their coming into the world brought great joy to us.

When we were expecting our first child, David, I was out on the road from Monday morning until Friday night. As it turned out, Margaret was a bit out on her timetable. I had decided to take an extra long trip, lasting two weeks, so that I might be able to loaf around home base for a week awaiting our first "bundle of joy". While I had left addresses, it wasn't until Saturday afternoon, on the way home, that I got my first message. Stopping at the Newcastle post office (open Saturdays in those years), I inquired of the postmaster, "Have you any mail for Dryden?" He looked at me and said, "Are you Dryden?" When I nodded affirmatively, he replied, "He came along Thursday morning and I told them to call him George." I frankly thought he was "nuts" until finally it dawned on me – "I'm a father!"

Well, it just seemed that every Ontario car was travelling #2 Highway that Saturday afternoon. It seemed to take hours to reach the Mount Hamilton Hospital, where I discovered mother and son doing exceedingly well.

I got chided so much about not being present at Dave's inaugural that my reputation was at stake when it came to Ken's arrival. I stuck close by, leaving phone numbers all over the place. Margaret snagged me at Grimsby and told me to get cracking. She wasn't fooling! I got her to Mount Hamilton Hospital with not too much to spare. When I arrived home, Dave was still not asleep, so I went upstairs and told him he had a baby brother. At first he did not say anything. Five minutes later he called downstairs, "Daddy, we're not going to have any more babies, are we?" Playing it safe, I said, "I don't know, Dave." He replied, "I sure hope not. Two is enough." This was one of the few times that Dave ever showed any jealousy toward his younger brother.

Ken hero-worshipped Dave when they were youngsters, and anything his older brother did was good enough for him. We never tire of telling the story of his christening. I was holding him when, all at once, he spotted his brother from the shoulder position and almost catapulted out of my arms while joyously exclaiming "Day-da". . . before his mother saved the situation and the ceremony by jamming a cookie into his mouth.

Unthinking people and the media frequently refer to Margaret and me as parents of Ken only. This hurts us, particularly when there has always been such a fine relationship between the boys. Indeed the two families' social lives are inseparable. For years Dave used to refer to his brother as "the Kid". On one occasion at least, when Ken strayed a little out of line, Dave bantered, "Listen Kid I made it before expansion and don't foget when there were only 12 goalies in the NHL. . . now with 21 teams anyone can make it!"

When Judy was expected, I was right on deck! When she was born, Dr. Murphy came out to the waiting room and announced, "You have a beautiful *daughter*!" I replied, "Harry, this is no time for fooling." Again he repeated, "I tell you, you have a beautiful daughter!"

Dr. Murphy was so right, and his early observation became even more pronounced as she went from babyhood to childhood to adulthood. She was the sunshine in our lives, but growing up in the shadow of her famous brothers was not easy for her.

The first sports event that I took Dave to was a basketball game at the Zion Church in Hamilton. He was about five years old and, midway through the game, coaxed me to take him home. I remember, when we got home, telling his mother that we might have a budding intellectual in the family but that the boy just wasn't interested in sports. And, I admit, I was disappointed. In later years when the dinner conversation in the Dryden household had revolved around sports, Margaret often reminded me of what I said. That was one prediction that turned out to be a hundred percent wrong.

I took Ken to his first sports event when he was four years old. We went to Varsity Stadium in Toronto to see a football game between Hamilton Tiger Cats and the Argos. He watched the game for ten minutes without saying anything. Then he turned to me and blurted out: "Daddy, why can't they stand on their 'wegs'?"

We moved from Hamilton to Toronto in February of 1949. Up until this time Dave had not shown much interest in sports. But this was soon to change.

One Saturday morning, when he was ten years old, we went to a lumber yard and bought some 2x4s. Then we got some chicken wire at a hardware store, brought it home and made a hockey net. It was the first and last thing I ever constructed in my life. The total cost was $6.60.

We set it up in the driveway in front of the garage door and the boys peppered a tennis ball at it for hours on end. And from that moment there didn't seem much doubt that Dave was going to play hockey and that he was going to be a goaltender.

We moved to a new home in Humber Valley Village in 1953. I had part of the backyard paved with red asphalt as a place for the boys to play. The original net was retired, and we ordered a pair of regulation goals made for us which we painted fire-engine red.

We must have inherited every kid in the neighbourhood! On Saturdays and holidays they would arrive early in the morning and stay till it got dark. Some of them brought their lunches. But if they didn't, Margaret always managed to find a few extra sandwiches to feed the hungry horde.

Ken at the time was only six years old and found himself playing with boys

Murray and Dave, 1946

Dave and the Hudson with its wooden bumpers

Dave, Margaret and Ken in Florida in 1952

almost twice his age. It was a pretty tough league and he often came out second best, but all through their athletic careers the boys always played with older age groups. I think this has been good for them. I feel it's better for a boy to be an average player in an older age group than a star in his own. He's not likely to get a swelled head that way. And it makes him work all the harder.

Because Dave was a goalie, Ken just had to be one too. To keep him from being killed, we outfitted him in a baseball umpire's chest protector and mask. And he insisted that he wear a Boston Bruins sweater. It was then his favourite team, which is sort of ironic, considering what happened in the 1971 Stanley Cup playoffs when, playing with the Canadiens, they dumped the Boston Bruins.

One day the grocery delivery boy arrived just as Ken was coming out, all togged out in his suit of armour. "Mrs. Dryden," he said, "a creature from Mars just came out of your basement!" It was a fairly apt description.

What with the flying pucks and tennis balls, the windows at our house took quite a beating. Finally, I covered them with iron grills and gratings. Our daughter, Judy, often said she felt she was sleeping in a jail.

While it was sometimes difficult to accept, Margaret and I nevertheless did not discourage our children from questioning our directions and decisions. We knew that somewhere down the road, if they did not have minds of their own, they would be trampled on.

One night, a few years ago, I came home rather late to find Margaret sitting up in bed and deep in thought. Asked what she was pondering, she replied, "I have been trying to recall any occasion that you laid your hands on our two boys. . . ." I laughed and said, "I can't remember ever having done it, but if you think I am going to start now, you're crazy!"

Margaret and I kept a scrapbook on the achievements of our three. In the early years, there's more about Ken as a baseball player than about his hockey career. It wasn't until he got to Cornell that Ken finally gave up baseball.

As you might imagine, with the boys playing several sports, there was bound to be a conflict. We had a rule in our household which worked out rather well. If there was a conflict, the first sport they had started to play took precedence. For instance, baseball rated over hockey, and hockey over basketball.

There was never much doubt in our family that education rated above everything else. And I don't take all of the credit. My wife Margaret was a school teacher before our marriage, and she impressed on the children at an early age that their school work came first.

One of the contentious issues that troubled us with our children, as they were growing up, was the matter of team sports programmes on the Sabbath. Below is a reprint of a letter I had written and which appeared in the *Globe and Mail*:

> "Citizens of Toronto who voted for Sunday Sports failed to see where it could interfere with Sunday morning church services. The safeguard of having organized games in the afternoon has been an illusion.
>
> "May I cite two factors of the present-day situation that bear out my contention. In preparation for any game, conservation of energy is essential, so the young athletes, instead of going to church or Sunday school,

A mid-50s family portrait: Ken, Margaret, Judy, Dave

sleep in and rest in order to be better prepared for the big game. Fathers and mothers must have an early lunch if they are to attend a 1:30 game, so again going to church is out. The problem is not Sunday sport itself but rather the *preparation* for Sunday sport.

"Another symptom of this creeping sickness of Sunday sport madness is the tremendous pressure on both coaches and boys to have a winning team. Sunday morning practices are set up and, if a boy is tempted to miss practice in order to attend church, he is in danger of being dropped from the team or, even worse, he is accused of letting the team down. This situation is particularly true of minor league hockey where practice facilities are limited and arena managers, anxious to pick up extra revenue, make the ice surfaces available for Sunday mornings.

"From the perspective of one who has been associated with leagues and teams in this community for thirteen years, I am grieved to see this trend towards the complete secularization of Sunday among our sports-minded youth. It is this writer's hope that league and team officials, in setting up their fall and winter programmes, will consider these problems and safeguard the spiritual as well as physical development of our youth.

"The many dedicated volunteer managers and coaches of minor league teams who set up practice sessions and games on Sunday mornings for our youth, are also unwittingly contributing to juvenile delinquency."

First Toronto Home,
132 Brentwood Road North

DAVE

February 3, 1962, is a date that we'll never forget in the Dryden household, for on that night Dave played his first game in the National Hockey League.

In those days, the NHL didn't insist that each team dress two goalies for each game as they do now. It was up to the home team to have a reserve goalie standing by in case the regular was injured.

Neighbourhood kids played
a lot of hockey using
the Dryden family net

Murray was manager and
sponsor of many teams over
the years. Here, he and coach
Russ Bowman flank goalie son Dave.

Dave and Sandra, 1962

While attending Teachers' College, Dave had been employed, on and off, for three years as the stand-by goalie at Maple Leaf Gardens, for which he was paid $10 per game. When, on that fateful night of February 3rd, Gump Worsley, the Ranger goalie, was injured in the first minute of the second period, Dave was called to the Ranger dressing room, where he picked up Worsley's sweater and got his instructions from coach Doug Harvey. He was told to pretend that it was just a junior game, but there wasn't much chance of that with 15 000 people in the stands!

In a story for *The Toronto Star*, Dave wrote: ". . . I sort of prayed I wouldn't be asked to fill in. If you go out there and blow an easy one before all those people, plus a television audience, you look pretty sad. The sweat was pouring off me while I buckled on the pads. . . . The butterflies were fluttering in my stomach as I walked out to the ice. . . . I'm accustomed to playing before three or four thousand and now there seemed to be a *million*!"

Dave went on to become the regular goalie for the Toronto Marlboros, and later played four games for the Buffalo Bisons of the American Hockey League, in which he allowed a total of just six goals.

He made his National Hockey League debut as a "regular" for the Chicago Black Hawks in 1965-66, playing 57 games – in which he had four shutouts and a goals-against average of 3.05. Next, it was on to the Buffalo Sabres and then the Edmonton Oilers of the World Hockey Association. He retired from professional hockey in 1980.

To quote from a Buffalo Sabres programme:

"The biggest moments for Dave Dryden don't always come when he's guarding the nets for the Buffalo Sabres. They happen in hospitals and guilds and homes where the youngsters gather in droves to hear the likeable Sabre goalie talk about the things he likes best – hockey and children. . . . Dave was twice a coach of a team in the floor hockey tournament in the Special Olympics. . . . He found it a real experience working with the retarded children."

Dave downplays his role in Ken's development as an athlete but he deserves much credit for it, as Ken points out. Dave's insistence, in those intense backyard games, that kid brother Ken, six years younger, be allowed to play or he himself would not, gave Ken the all-important chance to play against older boys and thus get a lot of action in the nets right from the beginning. This developed his experience and confidence.

Dave at 18, Judy (7), and Ken (12)

KEN

Ken attended Cornell University in the USA, where he emerged with "All-American" status. He later was called up from the Nova Scotia Voyageurs by the Montreal Canadiens Hockey Club at the end of the season – in time for the 1970-71 playoffs against Bobby Orr and the Boston Bruins. It seemed likely that Al McNeil, the Canadiens' coach, would go with the experienced Rogatien Vachon in the series – at least in the first two games in Boston. This would be a pretty tough spot for any goalie, especially a rookie. But, on the outside chance that he might get the starting assignment, I sent Ken a telegram to the Boston Gardens, which read: "RUIN THOSE BRUINS!"

McNeil decided to go with his rookie, and Ken had a very busy night, stopping 42 shots.

Here he sits beside goalie son Ken as a coach of the Humber Valley Hornets

Ken and Dave were active in many sports

Judy in athletic blazer at 16

The next game wasn't being televised in the Toronto area, so I had to rely on my car radio as I drove back and forth along Toronto's waterfront on a clear stretch of road to save my battery, which had been acting up. As I was cruising up and down my "drag strip", the Canadiens came back from a bad start to win 7-5. They went on to win the series 4-3, and, the morning after the final game, I received a telegram from Ken, which read: "BRUINS RUINED."

An exciting series that was, with the Canadiens unexpectedly winning the Stanley Cup. Ken was awarded the Conn Smythe Trophy and, the next year, the Rookie of the Year Award . . . all this while a law student at McGill University in Montreal. Ken and the Canadiens went on to win five more Stanley Cups.

I doubt if any player in the National Hockey League has ever gone from relative obscurity to instant fame as quickly as Ken did in the spring of 1971. One minute he was a minor league goalie – the next he was on a Stanley Cup championship team. With most athletes, fame is something that creeps up on them, but in Ken's case it happened all at once. Somehow he managed to adjust to it.

Ken was with Team Canada for the big 1972 showdown series with the Russians. What a thrill it was for me to be in Moscow for Team Canada's final-game victory – a memorable night for all Canadians.

Ken has since been named to the Hockey Hall of Fame and made a member of the Canadian Sports Hall of Fame.

In 1972, Dave coached at the Can-Am hockey school in Switzerland, and he has coached hundreds of boys in the off-season. In 1980-81, he was full-time coach of the Peterborough Petes of the Ontario Hockey League. He then went on to coaching goalers with the Detroit Red Wings.

A Special Education teacher, Dave is working towards his Master's degree.

By now a graduate lawyer, Ken worked with Ralph Nader on a water pollution project in Virginia, and with a hockey clinic in Vienna. In 1972, he was involved with a hockey film produced under the auspices of the President's Council on Physical Fitness. In 1977, Ken was appointed to Ontario's Advisory Committee on Confederation to advise the province on its relations with other provinces. Next came the writing of a book on hockey, followed by his appointment as Ontario's Youth Commissioner in 1984.

We tell Ken he was a "born lawyer" . . . that we never won an argument with him from the time he was four years old. And to think of all that money wasted on his formal training!

JUDY
Our daughter Judy played several games well. In her last year at Etobicoke Collegiate, she was elected president of the Girls' Athletic Association.

Judy's nursing career began at the Kingston General Hospital, following which she worked at the Queensway General and the Sunnybrook Medical Centre in Toronto. She had one year in Public Health studies at Windsor University, following which she headed out west to British Columbia to the Dawson Creek Hospital.

Judy enjoys her current public health career with the Vancouver school system. She and her husband, Kent Pearson, were recently blessed with their first child, Kathryn.

Both of our sons and their families live near us now. Dave and his wife, Sandra, recently purchased a home in Oakville. Their son Gregory, at 20, has just completed his second year in Finance at Queen's University, while his sister Debra, at 17, is at Oakville High School.

Ken and Lynda sold their home in Senneville, Quebec upon Ken's retiring from the Canadiens Hockey Club. They lived in Ottawa while Ken was completing his Law degree. They then spent one year in Cambridge, England before moving to Toronto and buying a home. Their children, Sarah, 10, and Michael, 7, are settled into the Ontario school system.

Looking back once more at those hockey days. . . . I was at the game at the Montreal Forum, in 1971, when Dave and Ken found themselves – for the first time – at opposite ends of the rink from each other. I sensed it was a more enjoyable spectacle for the fans and the media than for them.

Dave and Ken actually faced each other five times while Dave was with the Buffalo Sabres and Ken with the Montreal Canadiens. Never before nor since have brothers opposed each other in the NHL as goaltenders.

Dave, incidentally, was said to have the biggest feet in the NHL (wearing size 15 skates); and Ken, at 6'4", was considered the largest target ever to man a goal crease.

Both boys have demonstrated that it is possible to combine higher education with a successful career in the big leagues."

Aside from the preparation for another career when you are finished as a player, there is one other great advantage to combining education and hockey. Both Dave and Ken feel that gives you something to think about apart from hockey; and it can be a tremendous asset, as the player is too busy to dwell on the game just played or the one coming up.

Perhaps some day the colleges will provide most of the players for the NHL, just as they now do for football and basketball. This would be good for both the players and the sport.

Juniors play 60 games a year and make road trips as long as 300 miles in the east and much further in the west, which keeps the players out of school. They could play 30 games a year and still develop their skills. The NHL is currently forcing a young player to make his choice between hockey and education too early, and there is no reason he shouldn't be able to have both. Our two sons did, and I wouldn't have had it any other way.

In 1969, Dave was involved in an interesting programme at the Fitness Institute. The late Lloyd Percival helped him work on sharpening the reflexes, improving mental attitude and learning the feel of tension and of relaxation. "Tension just loads your muscles with electrical charges, leads you to make involuntary movements. Tension is adrenalin without action," Percival told Dave. He did not advocate naps on the afternoon of a game, which most players have, and he stressed ways of unwinding after a game. These tips have been useful to Dave in his coaching, as well.

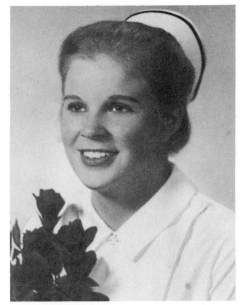

Judy as a graduate of Kingston General Hospital's Nursing School

Ken (Montreal Canadiens) and Dave (Buffalo Sabres) were goalies on opposing NHL teams

Margaret's mother, Dave's wife, Sandra, and son Gregory

Judy and Kent's wedding picture.

Murray with Dave and Sandra's children, Gregory and Debra

I was not what you could call a "passive fan" at a hockey game in which my sons were playing. People could not get over the antics I would go through. To hear them tell it, I did a striptease during the game. First, off came the overcoat, then the suit jacket, then I loosened my belt, took off my tie and finally removed my shoes. I'm also told that my lunging catches at an imaginary puck – and my footwork – were spectacular. I happened to remark one time that I didn't know what I would do if I ever had to play the shots at both ends of the rink – an innocent enough remark which later became the title for the book *Playing the Shots at Both Ends — The Story of Ken and Dave Dryden.*

While I would willingly subject myself to unbelievable agonies, Margaret, at the rink, behaved like a horse with blinders, making certain that she could not see what was happening at each end of the rink. Even at home, she would merely allow herself a periodic peek from a kitchen vantage point at the living room television set. One night I went all out, putting the two TV sets side by side with the sound turned off. I had the Leaf game on one, watching Dave perform for the Sabres on the other. I listened to Ken's game in Minnesota on radio, while perusing the *Financial Post* and chit-chatting with Margie. It wasn't long before she questioned her position on the totem pole!

Yes, the boys furnished a lot of pleasant memories for us during their hockey careers. One high point for me was the night in Buffalo, in 1972, when I was invited to participate in a between-period television interview on Sleeping Children Around the World. At the beginning of the game, as I stood for the national anthems in the packed auditorium, and looked down below and saw those two lads standing erect and motionless in front of their nets, *it was a proud moment for me!*

When SCAW took me away every winter, I missed the hockey excitement dreadfully. Often, I got back just in time for the Stanley Cup. However, in the spring of 1979, I had one really big "*hurrah*." I flew to New York on Saturday to see Ken and the Montreal Canadiens play the New York Rangers in the fourth game. Sunday morning I flew to Winnipeg to see the Edmonton Oilers with Dave in the nets play the Winnipeg Jets. On Monday I took a flight to Montreal to see the Canadiens win their fourth Stanley Cup in a row. When the game was over, I followed the media and others into the dressing room. As Ken removed his pads, in an aside to me, he said, "Dad, this is the last time I will be wearing these." A month later, he announced his retirement from the game.

Since the boys left hockey, the winters just have not seemed the same. . . .

Lynda and Ken, 1970.

Ken in net at 6 years in 1953 and his son Michael in the same location at 6 years, 30 years later

Murray and Margaret's grandchildren: Standing: *Debra;* Seated: *Michael, Gregory, Sarah, and baby Katie*

CHAPTER TEN

Viewpoint

Poverty   It's over fifty years ago, but I still have nightmares about personally-suffered episodes of poverty . . . makes me wonder how a child can endure the real thing day after day and night after night. . . .

In some countries, many are poor because they have too many children. Rapid population growth is more a result of poverty than a cause. Birth rates fall substantially only when the standard of living rises for the majority of people.

I will not soon forget attending a Kiwanis Club luncheon in Hong Kong when the president asked a member to pronounce Grace. His terse words were:

"Let us remember that four hundred will die of malnutrition by the time we finish this meeting."

A member of the World Health Organization, he knew whereof he spoke.

It is not all depressing, however. In the last thirty years, average life expectancy in the developing world has risen from 42 to 54 years. Literacy has jumped from 30 to 50%. Wouldn't it be great if similar gains could be made in the next 30 years?

Capitalism   I am a strong advocate of the Capitalist system, but only if it is disciplined. Unfortunately abuses are ever prevalent. Prices for goods and services more often than not are based strictly on what the traffic will bear. Back in my postwar construction days, a Scot and his son (Baird) taught me a lot in this regard. They operated Barton Stone, producing pre-cast window sills, toiling long hours, turning out a fine product. They gave good service and sold at a fair price. They prospered because they had no competition. No firm would oppose them because splitting the market at their prices would be uneconomical. Too their prices meant that most builders used their product not only on the front of their houses but also on the sides and rear. The home owners profited too as brick sills caused headaches with water seepage.

Apropos of all this I have on occasion been criticized for selling my Christmas trees lower than the competition. At the same time I found the 1984 price tags of $15-35 unconscionable and unchristian. Thirty years in the Christmas tree business and forty years in merchandising has taught me a lot. I still remember the ugly '60s when trees became a glut. Farmers could no longer afford to prune their trees and a vast majority of the plantations became jungles. Membership in our Association dwindled to the low thirties. It was only logical that a few years down the road trees would become scarce and growers would take

Family taking their
tree to the cashier

advantage of it. Prices were set at what they could get rather than what they cost. Consequently artificial trees were introduced and flourished. What hurt most was that a significant segment of the market stopped buying any kind of a tree and it is going to be difficult to turn them back on again when prices do become realistic. I prophesy that trees will be selling for six dollars by 1987. Our Association membership has grown by leaps and bounds to over 200 and the vast majority have been planting like mad. The exorbitant high prices have attracted the opportunists like a magnet. A few years ago when the industry was in the doldrums the Association lobbied and got a $30 000 annual grant from the Ontario Government to do several things, including the hiring of a manager. Recently that supplement was cut in half, causing many lamentations. It is my contention that, at present prices, we have no business receiving any subsidy that has to be paid for by the taxpayer. In reality we should be classified as S.I.W. cases (self inflicted wounds). But, when the millions of seedlings planted during the past four years commence coming on stream and prices plummet, mark my words the Association will be out there again asking for a full "handout".

World Population   Why have the populations of the World's cities continued to increase at a dizzy pace, while rural area numbers are constantly being decimated?

Why, for example, in countries like India and the Phillipines, do people leave the wide open spaces and flock into the human degradation of cities like Calcutta and Manila?

It has been explained to me that a crop failure in any land will trigger an exodus of a large segment of the populace into exploding urban regions, creating additional poverty and conditions for crime.

Lahore, Pakistan

Similarly, tens of thousands of young people, dazzled by the possibilities of the cities, leave the parental hearth each year to seek fame and fortune. A big percentage don't make it, become discouraged but too ashamed to go back home to face family and friends. . . . I know, because I went that route. . . .

Affluence   After a sumptuous Christmas Day dinner with Dave and his family in Edmonton in 1979, several of us elected for a lengthy walk. What did we come across but four very young children steering their new Christmas presents – junior-size snowmobiles – around an improvised track in a vacant area of a housing subdivision. Aside from the obscene capital expenditure, they were polluting the beautiful, bright crisp atmosphere of that day.

I guess snowmobiles are for the child who has everything. . . . I often think of that ugly scene when attempting to find even the simplest toy to place in a Slumber Kit with the child I am photographing.

Politics   How can political appointees live with themselves? They must know they are not qualified. Acceptance strictly on basis of money and prestige?

The Cabinet is considered the governing body of our Federal Government, although many electors maintain that it is the bureaucrats who call the shots. A recent survey of Prime Minister Trudeau's last Cabinet disclosed that nineteen – or over one half – were lawyers, seven were educationists, three were agriculturalists, and three were journalists. The rest were unidentifiable. I can only assume that they had gone directly into politics, possibly from university. Only two members came from the business world. Is it any wonder our country is hurting?

Prime Minister Mulroney's 1984 Cabinet of 40 members includes nine lawyers and nine businessmen.

And why does a Prime Minister constantly keep shuffling his Cabinet? Can it be likened to a coach who decides to trade his goaltender – or a manager firing his coach when the heat is on? More often than not, an "unknowledgeable" is slotted into the portfolio.

And the opposition critics – why, oh why can they not give the Government some credit for its legislation, instead of tearing apart every single programme of the party in power? If, only once in awhile, they would get up in the House and just say, "Bully for you!", it would not only increase their credibility but provide a real refresher for the electorate.

Economics   The Economic Council of Canada says, "An across-the-board enforcement of tough price-fixing legislation should be placed in the hands of an independent Competitive Practices Tribunal to better improve the consumer's bargaining position in the market place."

A recent inquiry at five international airline offices revealed that the "around-the-world" fare of each carrier was identical. Federal carrier Air Canada was one of them.

"And why beholdest thou the mote that is in thy brother's eye, but considerest not the beam that is in thine own eye?"

Business I dislike the practice by several service companies and businesses of placing the onus on the customer to contact them at the end of the year or conclusion of a contract; otherwise it is automatically renewed – and often at an increased rate. American Express is one example.

Religion Church worship in my life has meant a great deal to me. In the past ten years, when I have been travelling in the Near and Far East, I have wanted to seek out a Christian Church (any denomination) so as to worship Him. Often the service was in words I could not understand, but always the music came through as an international language.

The more I travel, and the more I see, the more I believe that Christianity is an anvil that will continue to wear out many hammers.

Thomas is my favourite disciple, as he was the only one of the twelve who had the "guts" to question Jesus.

Like most worshippers, I attend church for several reasons. One, as an example to my family. Another, I always feel better after I come out of the sanctuary – an exhilarated, indescribable sort of feeling. Thirdly, the secular part of my life tells me that if I listen to the word of God each Sabbath, as He keeps telling and reminding me how I should live, surely something will rub off on me. (Otherwise, the repetitious commercial advertising, costing millions, must be a total waste!)

I have asked my spiritual adviser to consider preaching more sermons on the theme "I believe", because, the other six days of the week, the media inundate me with the negative "Why I Should *Not* Believe."

Morality I would like to see less emphasis on *legality* and more on *morality*.

Music A musical thrill that I will long remember happened in the early '60s at a Keswick United Church Laymen's Conference. Following the Sabbath morning Communion in that ancient frame hall, on the birch-treed shore of glistening Lake Rosseau, 600 men rocked its foundations as they sang that wonderful old hymn *How Great Thou Art*.

Dance band leaders often puzzle me when they commence the evening programme with slow waltzes, gradually increasing the tempo as the night wears on. About the time you are "all in" except for your shoe laces, they will end up with "Tiger Rag" or something similar. Maybe they believe in reverse psychology.

Standing Ovations To me, this is a loathsome custom. It has sprung up mainly in the last few years, at first having been reserved only for an outstanding performance. This gave way to becoming as customary as the seventh-inning stretch. Of course there will always be a handful of people (relatives) who will jump up at the drop of a lousy speech and, like a cagey football lineman, carry the others offside. Recently, I have even noticed audiences giving standing ovations before the speech, so now we have reached the point of utter ridiculousness!

Education I always regretted not having a better education. At the same time, I was most thankful for having had three years of high school. My parents,

The Avonlea Church was a part of Murray's spiritual foundations

who had only Grade 6 and 7 schooling, made considerable sacrifices to enable me and my brothers and sisters to receive respectable schooling.

People often remark, "Education is not that important. One can supplement it with travel, experience, and the like." I hastily correct them, maintaining there is no substitute for formal education. Many a time I had to make sales presentations to architects, who would then ask me questions. Frequently I could not come up with an answer and, after stumbling and stuttering, would usually say, "I don't know the answer, but I will come back with it." Invariably, a few minutes later, going home in the car, the answer would come to me. Often, too, on finally coming to bed, Margaret would inquire of me, "Why are you so late in coming up from the office?" My usual reply, "It makes me angry to think I spent two hours on that speech or letter when, if I possessed a university training, it could have been accomplished in thirty minutes." It is my contention that, while one does not always retain what one learns at school, nevertheless formal schooling does teach one to think in a structured way.

Being hypersensitive about my academic shortcomings, I asked Margaret, as we started life together, to help me with grammar, composition and English in general. She would mentally note my "goofs" and speak to me about them later.

Often, when I would hear a speaker say something which seemed incorrect, I would scribble it down and discuss it later with my "tutor". This became a fetish, to the point that I even commenced to "jack up" my own parents. Years afterward, I was to regret this as I thought of the sacrifices made by them to give me a better education than they had had.

Instant Society   I am constantly quarreling with our instant society, and have almost reached the conclusion that anything fast isn't any good – e.g., instant coffee, instant ice, instant shade, instant potatoes, instant photography, instant marriages, etc. Why do people have to be so impatient?

Telephone Listings   Has anyone figured out the manner in which people list their names in the telephone directory? The more common the name, the more likely the use of initials, it seems, whereas names like Roman Zakrzewski will be spelled out in full. (Harold Brown, of course, is A.H. Brown!)

Communication Gap   We constantly hear chatter about this. I maintain that it should be termed "education gap". I found it difficult, at times, to relate to my parents. Our children – university "whiz-kids" – find it hard to get onto our wavelength.

Performance & Excellence   Good performance is character building. Over the years, we have had good, bad and indifferent youngsters delivering our daily newspaper, shovelling snow or cutting the lawn. If only they realized how important their performances were for the larger tasks that lay ahead. For more than a decade now, three carriers have seen that our morning paper reaches us before 7 a.m. in a satisfactory condition. I will be following the destinies of these conscientious young people. Their performances tell as much about their characters as an adult does by his or her behaviour on a golf course.

The Forties I am convinced that the forties are the best years in your life. One has had so much background of experience by that time and there are still bundles of energy to go, go, go. By the same token, it is probably the most dangerous decade. While people speak of the "trying thirties" – trying to raise a family, usually with little money left over for anything else – come the "fiery forties" and you sometimes have a few dollars kicking around in your pocket. That is the time when you want to get into something new – usually something you know little or nothing about.

Retirement While I have no quarrel with retirement, it strikes me that too many do it for the wrong reasons. I am sure you have heard friends say things like: "I've only got six months to go, and boy am I going to relax!" To that I say, "Relax and die" or "Use it or lose it." Although this may sound like double talk, I say too, "Take an early retirement providing it is practical – but don't let yourself die on the vine." Try to perform a useful function in society.

I always liken retiring with walking up stairs. Retiring at 60 can be compared to walking up the six steps in a split level, whereas retiring at 65 can be likened to walking up twelve steps in a two-storey house. It is the second six steps that often pluck you! At 60, there is a good chance that both you and your wife are still in reasonable health; but at 65, there is a strong probability that one or both of you will be incapacitated. Of course nowadays, one has to consider the ramifications of inflation when making this important decision. I guess one's only hope is an early demise.

Formal portrait of Murray in his 40s

Murray and Margaret with a slumber kit brought from Indonesia

Dreams   If you can't dream, forget it!

Sometime during the 1970s, on one of my trips to Africa, I attended a Methodist church service in Johannesburg. The theme of the sermon that day revolved around general criticism of "dreamers" in our society. Afterwards, I sought out the Minister and discussed the sermon at length. I told him that, while I subscribed to his thinking that we needed more "do-ers", we should not discount the importance of "dreamers" because they were often the forerunners of the "doing" population. Thousands would have "thrown in the towel" had they not been able to dream.

Naggers and Pessimists   Deliver me from these people – they are blights!

TV/Radio Interviews   Tuning in late on a splendid interview, I find it so disappointing when the guest's name is not repeated.

Noise Pollution   Raised decibels for radio and TV commercials are one of my biggest peeves. Whenever I have a few spare moments, I like to luxuriate in what I call my 4-shift contour chair. Frequently, Margie used to come to the door and shout to me downstairs to turn "it" down. Bouncing out of the chair every seven minutes or so, just to lower the volume, destroyed the whole value of the "contour". Letters to several of the offending advertisers only brought polite answers.

Finally, I thought of an idea to fix *them*. I went to the hardware store and purchased a rubber sleeve that fit snugly over the volume control button. Then I took this down to a bamboo shop and picked out a 9-foot pole with an end to fit tightly with the rubber sleeve. Now, when the commercial comes on too loudly, I just reach down to the pole resting on the floor beside my chair and give it about a half turn, choking off all advertising disturbance. During that new-found two minutes-plus, I enjoy reading or writing, which can total up to 15 minutes' peace every hour! This gimmick has been in use for over 12 years – the best $1.19 I ever spent.

Then there is the noise pollution of motorbikes, ill-functioning cars, raucous music, the practice of hammering commercials in department stores and some shops . . . all this is as devastating to us as is air pollution, yet it does not seem to get equivalent legislative attention.

Maple Leaf Gardens, in Toronto, for years has battered the fans before each game, and between periods, with an unmercifully long menu of coming events – all at an unbearable decibel count. Out-of-town sports scores, which appear on the scoreboard at each end of the rink, are even recited.

The Environment   I have, on occasion, made myself unpopular with acquaintances who have bird feeders. While I am not against feeding our feathered friends in winter, I am violently opposed to it at other seasons of the year. I tell these folk that they are cultivating socialism in the bird kingdom. More than once I have watched those big, fat, lazy birds gorging themselves – accepting the big "handout" at the feed trough, while lawns, trees, and such are being ravaged by bugs and insects. And now, since environmentalists, in their wisdom, have instigated legislation prohibiting the use of so many chemicals, it is doubly important that the birds get away from their lazy habits and commence performing the function our Lord intended for them.

Airline Fares   I have come to the conclusion that Airlines possess little or no compassion! Fares seemingly are promulgated on the basis of what they can extract from the customers, not on what the service actually costs. For example, domestically, why is that if I want to pay a friendly visit to my daughter in Vancouver, and book 14 days in advance, the fare is $299? But, if the trip becomes an emergency, then I am clobbered $778 for the same trip? Where is the morality? To eliminate possible abuses, I would advise using strict guidelines, such as those required for passport applications.

Highway Facilities (or Bring Back the Tourist)   As one who has travelled this continent extensively, it is hard to understand some of the experiences I have had with food and gas services on our fast highways.

The oil companies, in their anxiety to procure outlets for their product, offer fantastic bids for these locations. An almost captive clientele pays up to 10 percent higher for gas and 25 percent more for meals. This makes for disgruntled patrons. People travel these limited-access highways because they are in a hurry. The time gained on the highway is frequently lost in the restaurant and service station.

The highway facilities are often our United States guests' first and last impression of Canada. Conceivably, some of the high rental fees coming into the Department of Highways are being spent by the Department of Tourism to encourage our southern neighbours to sample Canadian hospitality. Improved dining and gas services on high-speed arteries would help bring tourists back to Canada.

Golf   How many golfers experience horrendous difficulty in navigating the first hole! My suggestion is to throw out the offering of a "mulligan" on the first tee, call it the "mulligan hole" or "the 19th" (or even the "minus-1") – in other words, change the first hole to a practice hole.

Swimming   Having been raised on a farm in Manitoba, there was little opportunity for swimming; consequently, I never learned to swim properly, which I very much regret. During my seventy plus years, I have had some narrow escapes in water, indeed almost drowning on three occasions – once when I was about twenty years old, a second time in 1974 in the Caribbean, when an undertow caught hold of me and Margaret tried desperately to enlist aid from others on the beach (they did not accept that I was in trouble), and a third time at our son Dave's cottage on Peninsula Lake near Huntsville.

The family had gathered at Dave's cottage for a few days to celebrate our 40th wedding anniversary. I was swimming alone while the others were preparing a barbeque supper. I had gone a long way out, to shoulder depth, then began to swim parallel to the shore. When I attempted to touch down for a rest, I found that I couldn't touch bottom. Fighting to get back on the top of the water, I struggled a few more strokes toward shore but again could not touch bottom. I waved

Serving the public, tourists or locals, is always a pleasure

frantically and hollered but the wind was unfavourable. Finally, not a second too soon, they got my message and Dave led the rescue squad. . . .

Sports Predictors　　Open season should be declared on all of these so-called experts. So seldom do they bat '500', yet they continue to analzye and psycho-analyse players and teams for days before major events.

Pro-Athlete Commercials　　They are usually so amateurish that the merits of the product sound totally unconvincing. It always amazes me that advertisers continue to use athletes for advertising.

The All-Round Athlete　　The era seems to be coming to an end. Professional sports have so extended the seasons for financial reasons that now we have hockey, baseball, basketball and football with clashing schedules.

Athlete of the Year　　At the collegiate level the award is now of dubious merit. The biggest percentage of the athletes, in an age survey, are 19 and 20 years of age. I say that any student who hangs around collegiate until the age of 20 should not be considered for this award. Bear in mind that the average student is out at 18 and the brighter ones at 17. It always strikes me as unfair to see so many Grade 13 students, 17 years old, with above-average athletic prowess, lose out to a classmate three years older – and three years' brawn on a football line means a lot. I suggest that recognition be given those students best combining athletics and scholastics.

NHL Hockey Schedule　　We all hear fans comment and complain about the length of the National Hockey League schedule, and the playoff set-up that allows 16 out of 21 teams to qualify for the Stanley Cup Trail, which stretches the playoffs an additional six to eight weeks.

The owners reply: "Our arenas are packed – the fans must like it or they would not pay."

But I ask, "Do the *fans* pay?" More often than not, as in the season's subscription schedule, the tickets are held by commercial firms and their expense can be an income tax write-off.

Companies subscribe because tickets for professional sports events are something they can give that their customers cannot obtain on their own. So the bottom line is: "It is you the Taxpayer who pays for immense player salaries and extended schedules."

Fan Behaviour　　Hockey fans, and others, have a habit that puzzles me. When the home team scores, they litter the ice or playing area with debris, which of course delays the game. By the time the game resumes, their team may have "cooled out" and lost its momentum. I'm certainly not advocating throwing things on the ice but . . . if they must do it, fans would help their team more if they littered the ice when the visiting team scored.

Sportsmanship　　I frequently recall an act of sportsmanship that happened one night in 1959 at Maple Leaf Gardens when Dave was playing Junior A with

Official puck from the National Hockey League

the St. Michael's Majors. They had just completed a long and, at times bitter, playoff series with St. Catharines "Teepees". When the boys lost the final game, there was the usual line-up at centre ice with the losing gladiators quickly performing the customary perfunctory handshakes before escaping to the shelter of their dressing room. On this occasion, I saw Terry O'Malley linger until most of the fans had left the building. He more than made certain that he shook every opponent's hand, pausing to say a few words of congratulations. He was the last player to leave the ice and I, for one, was tremendously impressed. "How a man plays the game shows something of his character – how he loses shows all of it."

Canada's Image Abroad   I will never forget that night of the Canada-Russia hockey final in 1981. Losing by a lopsided 8-1 score did not upset me as much as the deportment of our team before the puck was dropped to start the game. During the playing of the two National Anthems, the Soviet players all stood erect and motionless, their goaltender Tretyak bareheaded. Our players, on the other hand, slouched, shifted around, gazed at the crowd, and chomped gum through both anthems, while Liut never even removed his goalie mask! I was thoroughly ashamed at our team's lack of discipline for the sake of a few short minutes . . . and in front of 100 million people! Yes, I am sensitive about anything which tarnishes our Canadian Image. . . .

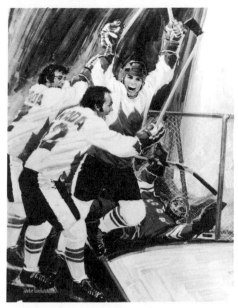

Canada-Russia hockey final in Moscow 1981

CHAPTER ELEVEN

Sleeping Children Around the World (SCAW)

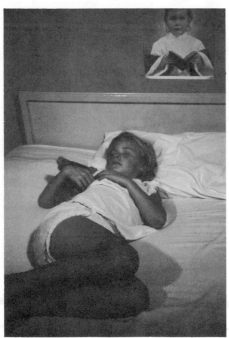

Judy asleep inspired a dream that was realized with Sleeping Children Around the World

HOW IT ALL BEGAN

I had a habit of checking on our daughter, Judy, asleep in her room, before I turned in every night. On one particular occasion, in 1961, when Judy was nine years of age, I discovered her sleeping in a most unusual position. I went and got her mother, then my camera, and took several shots of our child "in limbo", so to speak. I subsequently took many more pictures of Judy asleep, then of our next-door neighbour's son, Paul Brehaut. I went on to photograph Gregory Dryden, our grandson, and then a nephew.

After netting children of a number of friends, I commenced lining up photo sessions with some of my customers. Arriving about seven o'clock, I would take candid shots of the child in his or her night attire – first playing, eating, or reading, in order to capture the personality of the child. Later I would slip into the sleeping child's bedroom, often sitting in the dark for upwards of two hours waiting for my subject to turn to interesting positions.

At that time, in the construction business, I was dealing with the "melting pot" of the world; while engaged in these countless photographic sessions, I soon realized that Dutch, Yugoslav, German, Indian, Philippine and other children had the same sleeping customs and habits as Canadian children. How much more exciting to take the pictures in their native habitat!

It had been several years since I had had a holiday, so I decided to go to Europe and photograph more sleeping beauties! I wrote out the purpose of my mission, taking some 1500 words (I was never known for brevity!) to be translated into the language of the various countries. However, upon discovering that this little exercise was going to cost $75 for each translation, I elected for German and French, along with English, and had the typed transcripts multigraphed. I then prepared a questionnaire to cover all information concerning the sleeping habits and customs of each child. Armed with these, plus picture release forms and accompanying brand-new Canadian $1 bills, I set out for Europe in May 1964.

While I had been president of branches of two international organizations – Kiwanis and the YMCA – and had made several acquaintances during the war, I nevertheless had to knock on a lot of doors, with a good percentage of turn-downs. Upon analysis, I wonder what my reaction would be should someone from Mesopotamia want to prowl around *my* child's bedroom! Fortunately, my sales background helped me to accept the rebuffs.

After these trips, my box score read: 132 bedrooms in 28 countries. I would dearly love to go back to see these original subjects sometime! I even took pictures in Russia, although I had to go back a second time. They were indeed suspicious of me – to relate this tale would require a whole chapter.

Remember, I was taking pictures principally of middle-class children in Europe and Asia. I did not want to downgrade any country. We have children from all socio-economic levels in Canada, too.

After collecting all these pictures, I had hoped to interest some publisher in putting them into a book. In 1968, I took some of the family down to New York for a week between Christmas and New Year's. While they sampled the excitement of the city, I canvassed a few of its leading publishers. The results were hardly encouraging. The closest I came was with Grosset & Dunlap, who indicated interest only if I could bring the magic number up to fifty countries. The mere thought of covering another twenty-two countries wearied me – I should live so long!

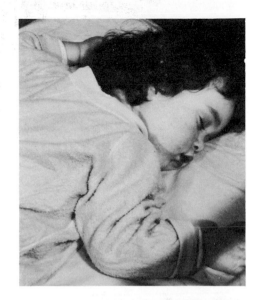

THE BIRTH OF SCAW

It was the following December, while I was driving home from one of our Christmas tree farms in a blinding snowstorm, that the question flashed at me: "Why not *beds* for children in the developing countries?" While I had been taking the pictures of middle-class children, I had also seen the plight of poor children. I was so excited about the idea that I could hardly wait to unload it on Margaret!

The following day, I telephoned Colonel Tripp, Chief Secretary at the Salvation Army in Toronto, asking him for an appointment to discuss my idea. He felt the plan was of sufficient interest to follow through. We drafted a letter and the Colonel mailed copies of it to branches in ten countries. When we received positive acknowledgements from six countries, we were on our way! SLEEPING CHILDREN AROUND THE WORLD, a brand-new registered Canadian charity, dedicated to the Third World's children, was born. . . .

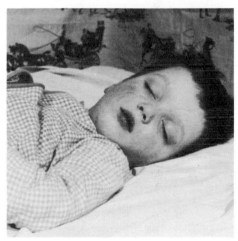

Belgian children asleep

Not wishing to involve a lot of people before we were certain that the programme had merit, we decided to take $3000 of our personal funds and send $1500 to the YMCA at Bombay and $1500 to the Salvation Army at Bandung, Java. In each case, the money was to be used surreptitiously in making up one hundred kits; I would then go along in August to distribute and photograph the children asleep in their beds. We made up labels in the names of our family, friends, and associates, and these labels later were affixed to the bottom of the little mattresses.

I had some wild and wonderful experiences on this initial trip . . . too many to mention, but we were never discouraged – just cognizant of the fact that a lot of tinkering with the organizational mechanics would have to be done.

D. MURRAY DRYDEN
Founder and Director
SLEEPING CHILDREN AROUND THE WORLD

28 Pinehurst Crescent
Islington, Ontario, Canada M9A 3A5   Tel. (416) 231-1841

Insisting that each child had to be asleep to be photographed created difficulties in the orphanages where they lived. First of all, the children were so excited at getting into what, in most cases, was their first bed, that they had trouble getting to sleep. We would go away and drink coffee but soon discovered that one can drink only so much coffee. Working with oil lamps or flashlights, stifling heat, mosquitoes, and with separating the prepared gummed labels, our patience was severely tried.

When our distributions reached into the thousands, we had to sacrifice our insistence on every child being asleep when we photographed them. It was a great pity as *there is nothing more beautiful and peaceful than a sleeping child*!

First SCAW Distribution   This took place in St. Crispin's Home, an Anglican Church orphanage in Puna, India, on the night of August 17, 1970, with a distribution of 50 kits.

It was a tense, but at times hilarious, experience. At one juncture, just when all 50 pairs of eyes seemed to be really closed, a huge green frog appeared in the beam of the flashlight and hurdled over the prostrate forms – triggering giggles from the Sisters. Soon the whole room was in a state of eruption. . . . Colonel Pilley and I still recall that at Bandung everyone was in Slumberland when a distressed little voice cried out, "Pottie!" or, rather, whatever the word was in her language.

Thirteen years later, when again distributing kits in Puna, I was reminded of our first distribution there. Of course, those children from 1970 had long since gone, but it was a great thrill to return, this time with Dr. Gordon Brown on his first such encounter with the children.

Extending our programmes from orphanages and hostels, we began to distribute to more needy children in their own homes, i.e., one-room shanties.

While distributions in main cities would be much easier, we find that children in the rural sections suffer the most deprivation, so we put much of our effort there. We invariably have to do a lot of planning to land the slumber kits in these areas.

Transport   Transport is a real bugbear. The labels, alone, weigh ten pounds per thousand and present another obstacle to us on our flights; however, with all materials for the kits purchased locally, no transportation costs are incurred in this respect.

Inventory   The inventory is usually placed in a building, school, or church with a guard on duty. Recipients are selected by the agency (Salvation Army, Jesuits, Church of South India, Kiwanis, Rotary, YMCA, International Boys' Town, etc.) and are chosen strictly on the basis of need. Less than 5 percent are Christian. They are given tickets with the distribution location, date and time. It is not unusual for them to have to walk for up to five hours, leaving mountain homes at 3:00 a.m. After the photograph session, they are each given a mug of hot milk and a handful of flat rice; they then leave, clutching their kits, for the long homeward journey.

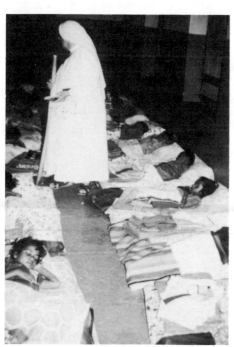

First distribution took place at St. Crispin's Home in Puna, India in August 1970

*In Nairobi, Kenya,
Colonel Walter of the
Salvation Army helps with
a load of kits bound for
Tororo, Uganda*

The country's economy is helped by our practice of buying the materials locally, and we employ many unemployed in the making up of the kits. As well, we often feed the workers while they are producing the kits.

We believe that if a bed can be provided to take the child's mind off hunger for a few hours each night, it helps conserve his or her diminished energy for the day ahead.

Over the years, we have "plugged the holes" and, today, we have a system that is greatly simplified and applicable in almost every country serviced.

"Why beds?"   People frequently ask me this. I usually answer by asking another question: "Have you ever been involuntarily without a bed for a period of time?" In every instance they have replied that they have not. I go on to say that they would never have asked that question if they had.

"Why not food?"   Margaret and I have chosen this programme of Slumber Kits because it is something that we can handle, whereas we could never administer a food programme. Too, there is no overlapping. Insofar as we know, no other charity supplies beds. Overlapping can be almost as much a sin as doing nothing.

Margaret and SCAW   Margaret is a strong arm of SCAW. She works as hard as I do, and not only does she have the dull but vital job of "minding the store" when I'm away, she records all the donations, answers letters, and is responsible for all the labels and other tedious administrative details. She is typical of the finest type of Canadian volunteer who is found behind the scenes of many organizations working quietly, reliably and not asking for recognition. She can march, and does, "without the band".

*Stockpile of materials in India, to be made
into sheets and mattresses*

Margie is helped by some 30 volunteers, many of them senior citizens from our church. Our home often resembles Union Station as those kind folk flit in and out, giving a few hours whenever they can. The dining room table is rarely available for entertaining.

It took the Beta Sigma Phi Sorority, Preceptor Alpha Upsilon of Etobicoke, to honor Mrs. Dryden by naming her "Woman of the Year". Thursday evening, April 28, on the occasion of the Greater Toronto City Council of Beta Sigma Phi's celebration of their 52nd Founder's Day. Mrs. Dryden was presented with this significant award "for morally supporting her husband – while he was in private business; while he was President of the Kiwanis Club and of the YMCA; in the encouragement of their children in their careers and encouraging the founding of Sleeping Children Around the World; for her personal contribution to humanity through her 33 years as a member of the United Church Women of Humber Valley United Church and a member of their choir for 22 years, and for her unselfish dedication to the needy children around the world."

from an article by Betty Coulter

Margie also helps me immeasurably in that she gives me hope, soothes my ruffled feathers and reminds me that – no matter what the frustrations of the day – the sun will rise again tomorrow. I couldn't run SCAW without her. . . .

Travel   We have never found a way whereby two can travel as cheaply as one, although I did take Margaret on a distribution in Haiti in 1973, and to Korea, the Philippines and Indonesia in 1979. I wanted her to see the other side of all this.

116

Although I tried hard to pick the spots for her, and in spite of having a stronger handle on her emotions than I have, she nevertheless broke down on two occasions. The poverty and human degradation crushed her! When she apologized, I told her to forget it . . . the same thing happens to me if I absorb the mental punishment for more than a week at a time.

When travelling together, Margaret and I never sit together on the plane. We arrange aisle seats across from each other. If we have interesting seat-mates, we ignore each other; if they are "lost causes", we converse with each other.

Tax-free?   Travel for SCAW could be income-tax deductible, I agree, but I continue to be dead-set against this. I feel that this practice is so overdone already; besides, I feel it is important that this work be totally given. Perhaps I can best express what I feel about this by quoting the late John F. Kennedy:

"Ask not what your country can do for you but what you can do for your country."

The words "tax deductible" are the most used/abused . . . .

The Photography: The Children Face-to-Face   We attempt to get a little cultural aspect as a background, usually by doing the photography outdoors with as interesting a backdrop as we can organize. Sometimes we experience difficulty in getting the children to smile into the camera, which must make some donors wonder if "their" child really appreciates the gift. On the 1983-4 trip, we actually photographed 11 000 children!

*Murray taking pictures at
San Juan in the Philippines*

117

*Three children with
their sleeping kits
in Indonesia*

A word of explanation: these little souls are usually scared stiff of *me*. They imagine all sorts of things about to happen; some take me for a doctor who is about to give them the big needle. My different language and skin colour also contribute to tension.

I have tried all sorts of ways to animate them – making grimaces, using toys and face masks – but discovered, on my last trip, that singing some of the "oldies" like "Old McDonald Had a Farm", "The Bullfrog on the Bank" and "The Smoke Goes Up the Chimney Just the Same," etc., simply broke them up! As they cannot possibly understand the hilarity of the words, it must be the quality of my voice which provokes the laughter.

Three kits are laid out with three children posed in them, and sometimes a parent or other family member standing behind them. We take one shot and have three prints made for the three donors. The "love label" is held by each child and, after the picture is taken, that label is affixed to the kit.

A Japanese Airlines traveller and donor remarked, one time, "When you receive that photograph, it is a sobering experience. . . ." Another donor told me, "As you photograph that child, my eyes see the child, too, and I reach out to him. . . ."

(Do you know what it is like to give for years never knowing for sure what your money is doing? Then for the first time getting a picture to show you? I had to blink away the tears. Many, many thanks for taking the time to send me pictures.)

Itineraries   My trip every year is like a jigsaw puzzle. I spend hours, like a general, poring over the maps of the world to plot my itinerary.

Do you know what it is like to give for years never knowing for sure what your money is doing? When for the first time getting a picture to show you! I had to blink away the tears. Many, many thanks for taking the time to send me pictures.

For example, communications and transport for Bangladesh are rough. We could get air reservations over to Jessore, 170 miles from Dacca, but not back in time to connect for our flight to Calcutta and on to Manila. By car, 8-10 hours are required, depending on ferries. A civilian bus takes 10-12 hours. By train, it's two days – yet the flight is only 12 minutes!

Agencies   If an organization overseas sits on our mail, this greatly hampers our efficiency. I *must* get to each destination when I say I'll be there, and the church or agency must have everything ready for my arrival so that we can process two or three hundred beds a day. It is just too costly if I have to wait around for them to finish their part of the work. Delays tie my airline schedule in knots and my arrival schedules at the next locations are ruined. Yet, I must never forget that SCAW is dealing with people who are often doing their best and who have few of the facilities we take for granted . . . . In the recent guidelines for agencies, I told them, "Remember, I can handle 16-hour days – even if I am in my seventies."

Commitments by us to agencies are usually made in August or September, at which time we suggest that they explore the market for the best prices in materials, with the money to go out from our end in December.

The kits are always made up in the country of distribution, and must be ready for January, February or March, depending on the distribution schedule.

Going-Away Gear   Besides my heavy overcoat, rubbers are part of my gear. For several years, I would ditch them somewhere in the Far East, usually to a rubbers-less Indian facing the upcoming monsoons. However, with rubbers at $10 per pair now, I have been lugging them around the world. Imagine my consternation, last year, upon leaving the Philippines for Indonesia, to find my rubbers on the missing list. Upon arrival at the Salvation Army headquarters in Jakarta and relating this story to Captain Frans, he disappeared – only to reappear in a few minutes with a pair that I apparently had left four years earlier.

To Margie with love – from Johannesburg   I should say that both Margie and I have a thing about *hats* – we love them!

This story began in Johannesburg in 1974. It was my first visit. In the evening, I fell into my usual habit of taking a long walk to see what was going on. In a milliner's window was an elegant, fine straw hat in the spotlight, and I knew that was just the hat for my girl! But how could I possibly carry it home halfway around the world? It was too big, for one thing. I kept passing by and looking at that hat. . . .

When I finally went back, determined to buy it, it had been sold. The fact that somebody else liked it, too, made me want it even more. The manageress and I tried everything to find another, without success. Then my luck changed. The manufacturer agreed to make one especially for me and even deliver it to my hotel at no extra charge for the rush job.

Getting it home was another story. Two different Customs officials, at Perth and Auckland, insisted they had to spray the straw hat because of the prevalence of hoof and mouth disease. I had a tough time talking them out of this.

Margaret's notorious hat from Johannesburg

I thought that I was home safe on the last lap, but an attendant with frosty blue eyes asked what was in "the box", and stated that I could not carry this extra piece of luggage into the cabin. I explained about my impulsive moment of idiocy in making this purchase, and that now that I had gotten it three quarters of the way around the world, I intended to complete my mission – ". . . so don't break my heart now!" She smiled, relented and then asked, "What will you do if she doesn't like it?" I replied, "Then I'll have to trade her in!"

And so I landed home with the elegant hat and Margie was delighted!

In 1980, when I returned to Johannesburg, I traced the man who had made it all possible and took him a photo of Margie posing under the blossoming apple tree in our garden and, of course, wearing *the hat*. He agreed that they were meant for each other.

THE KITS

While the kits are still $25 Canadian, in reality they cost $28 – but we have been hesitant, in these times, to raise the price, although many donors do send us the $28 now. We try to make up the difference with bank interest and our other fund-raising ventures. On 10 000 beds, the difference of $3 amounts to $30 000.

Postal rates have rocketed since we started SCAW. In fact, the rate in 1984 went from 30¢ to 48¢ for printed matter (50 grams) in Canada. It was a dreadful shock to learn that, while Canada Post claimed to have held the line on postage rates, there no longer was a 2nd class classification. It doesn't seem to make sense that one can send a letter to New Zealand for the same rate as one of equivalent weight to Hamilton, only a few miles away. We gladly accept stamped, self-addressed envelopes from any who wish to include them in correspondence with us.

We insist on every cent of every donation being spent on the kits. There are no hidden costs of any kind – and nothing is siphoned off for administration, publicity, travel or even photography expenses. We personally police each of these areas.

The *basic kit* consists of a small mattress with two rubber sheets – one to go under the mattress and one over the top to protect it – cotton sheets, pillow and cases, a blanket, a mosquito net and pyjamas or equivalent. If it is a cold climate, we supply an extra blanket and possibly skip the mosquito net.

Occasionally, if there is a serious problem with rodents, such as rats, in an area, we try to find an extra $15 to $20 for a steel cot rather than have the child sleep on the ground or the floor. There is some variation from country to country.

In Bombay, Dr. Shirish Sheth, a Rotary Governor there, engineered a unique kit which even included a "tongue scraper", which is as popular as a tooth brush in India.

In Central Celebes, Major Victor Tondi of the Salvation Army included SCAW T-shirts among the 15 items in their kits. The shirts had "Sleeping Children Around The World" on the front and "SCAW" on the back. Major Tondi remarked about the expression of unbelief on the faces of the first couple of children in the line-ups to collect their kits. Apparently they expected, at the

Child (supposed to be asleep) in her bed and pyjamas, Indonesia

most, a mattress and a pillow, but never in their wildest dreams a kit containing fifteen items.

In the Punjab in Pakistan, it was the first time the children had had anything new and they could not believe the kit was theirs to take home. Indonesians, in particular, find it difficult to understand that Canadians would give them beds for their children without wanting anything in return.

In the Philippines, poor families sleep together, so we decided to supply one child in each family with an 8' x 6' piece of good quality cocoanut matting, sheets, blanket, pillows, pyjamas, and a huge, heavy-duty, family-sized nylon mosquito net, which came in brilliant colours. Sometimes, as many as *eight* people can curl up comfortably under this protective netting. We decided to try this new method in Indonesia as well, even though it meant revamping our distribution methods.

Nothing is wasted by the local people who do the sewing in various areas. Left-over cuttings are sometimes even made into patchy sheets and given to mothers for wrapping their naked babies. One agency told us: "The programme has a long life, causing ripples in the society, as rugs, too, are made with the kit cuttings for the still more underprivileged." Some medical clinics even use the wax paper backing from the name labels for distribution of ointments. *Nothing is wasted.*

Team of local poeple making parts of the kits at one centre in India

RECIPIENTS

Thus far, 85 500 children in 18 countries have been furnished with kits. These countries have an Earnings per Capita of $300 a year or less (many under $100). Culture, climate and inflation must be primary considerations in selecting the countries for distribution. Inflation prevents us from having a programme in many countries. We have to decide whether we put one child into bed in Sâo Paulo, Brazil, or three children in Port-au-Prince, Haiti.

THE DONORS

From Canada comes 80% of our funds, while 15% comes from Australia and 5% from the USA.

Who are the donors? 75% of the donors are what we call "One bedders". They contribute each year – some in memory of a loved one, others as a congratulatory gesture toward a friend or family members, others for other reasons. Many are Charter donors, pensioners, widows often sending $5 at a time toward one kit a year. After such sacrifice, it is no wonder we do not countenance waste.

We continue to receive anonymous donations from folks who go to great pains to wipe out any possible chance of our tracing them, so we can't express our appreciation nor acknowledge their gifts. We respect and applaud these donors, but we urge them not to send donations in cash.

It is especially gratifying that such donations are made by people who care – not by governments, who often give with one hand and take away with the other.

Some donors tell us that they have special albums in which they place the photograph of their new child (or children) each year. The pictures sometimes even find their way into purses or onto refrigerator doors . . . .

Each kit is identified, when possible, by a donor card — here for Maple Leaf Gardens founder Conn Smythe.

Donors live in many different countries.

FUNDING

SCAW is a made-to-order project for church outreach programmes and, as most service clubs have active international committees, we can furnish a safe and useful outlet for a portion of their welfare funds. We provide the so-necessary follow-through, as we work co-operatively with these organizations in the Third World. In 1984, we distributed 4000 kits through the Salvation army, 3000 through Rotary, 2500 through Kiwanis and 1500 through the Canadian Jesuits. They were responsible for making up the kits, selection of the most needy children and providing the necessary workers at the time of distribution.

Besides service clubs and churches, support comes from day schools, Sunday Schools, Girl Guides, Brownies and the corporate community.

A goodly percentage of our funds comes from schools. Clare Walsh, a teacher at Forest Hill School in Renforth, N.B., inspired her Grade 3 class, back in 1972, to have a fudge sale – raising and sending us $37.03 for our first "school donation". Every year since, they & Glen Falls School have donated increasing amounts.

Harbord Collegiate in Toronto raised $1000 and the principal told me that SCAW has "grabbed" the students – much as they, with their enthusiasm, "grabbed" *me*. In fact, I came away from that school just *bouncing* – not only from their SCAW fund-raising music presentation but from the joy of seeing so many representatives of so many nationalities working together on a SCAW project!

When telling Rotarian Bud Crookes, following a talk to the Don Mills Rotary Club, that several schools were supporting us, and that we had only just skimmed the surface of that potential, Bud too, felt it was a "natural" for schools. He came up with the idea of enclosing a large picture postcard of SCAW children in a mailing to all Canadian schools. He had a business contact with an American firm, Science Research Associates. Through their president, Mr. Stanley Reid, they offered to distribute these for us – another example of fine corporate citizenship.

This school mailing really got SCAW rolling. A second mailing was again very productive, and we estimate that $57 000 resulted from these two campaigns (nearly 3000 beds). It is hoped that more schools will support SCAW in the future.

The greatest success story belongs to the Father C.W. Sullivan Catholic School in Brampton, Ontario. An article written by Trent Frayne, appearing on the sports page of the *Toronto Sun* provided the trigger. The principal, Brian Martin, had been concerned about the ugly commercial inroads on the celebration of Christmas and was looking for a Christian focus on Christmas. When he read the Frayne article on SCAW, he saw a way of eliminating all gifts to his staff and among pupils.

In four years, this school donated $44 000 – by far the largest contributions in our fund's history! Don't ever sell this younger generation short. And what a display of pictures of *their* Third World children appears on the walls of the school lobby! The follow-up story was reported by Michael McAteer, Religion Editor of the *Toronto Star*.

Special individual donors have been the Goddards, who have bedded 100 children each year since 1972. And then there are those enthusiastic folk at Renforth who throw a super Hallowe'en Dance every October and send a cheque to SCAW. And there are others including service clubs, from whom we receive much appreciated support.

Receipts from our annual Family Day at our Christmas Tree Farm – the "Christmas Tree Drag" – continue to make this our major fund-raiser.

In 1983, we acted as "Agent" for our son Ken's bestseller, *The Game,* about his hockey career. This added over $5000 to the fund. We intend that this book you are now reading will also help our fund-raising.

Back in 1973, I spent several weeks in the National Archives at Ottawa, the Library of Congress in Washington, newspaper morgues in Detroit, Chicago, New York, Toronto, Winnipeg, Saskatoon, Regina, Salisbury, Johannesburg, Auckland, Perth, the British Museum in London and national libraries in Dublin and Edinburgh. When I found an item of interest, I took the date and had a microprint made of the page. After bringing these home, I cut out what I wanted and then had three typists (with magnifying glasses – it was a punishing exercise for the eyes) type 500 000 words dating back to 1755. Out of this material I selected 100 000 words, plus old pictures, put them in a tabloid and called it *Nostalgia.* Besides providing needed exposure, the $1 newspaper raised some money for Sleeping Children Around the World.

Every five years, the two-day Dryden Reunion is held at Cambridge, Ontario. At the 1975 and 1980 Reunions, I was asked to speak at the Sabbath morning services. The generous collection was turned over to SCAW.

We owe so much to the TV programme "100 Huntley Street". I was privileged to appear on their splendid programme on 3 July 1980. For the following

Donors from Rotary and Kiwanis have been generous.

three weeks, we were almost swamped with the most beautiful letters resulting from this daily presentation directed by Reverend David Mainse. The gifts in these letters made it possible for us to provide over 2000 kits. Again, on 25 November 1981, I was asked to appear and to give a progress report. The viewers for that show responded to the tune of another 450 kits. You can understand how deeply indebted we are to "100 Huntley Street".

Canadian companies help us with supplies, for which we are very grateful. It has almost reached the point where I throw my hat in first when I go to pick up these supplies!

A number of firms and individuals donate products and services to SCAW – from films and batteries to printing and accounting services. We use, as much as possible, recycled stationery and appreciate these donations, as well as envelopes.

Our newsletters, since 1982, have been printed at the Bob Rumball Centre for the Deaf. We are given good service and a fine job and the contract helps their employees.

The media have been most helpful – so important when we have no funds for advertising, nor do we have a mailing list (don't believe in them). We never nudge, remind, nor hammer our donors. Many are giving to worthwhile charities in addition to SCAW.

Telling the SCAW story to groups has been our most effective method of publicizing the programme. It is not uncommon to average three or more presentations a week to schools, service clubs and church groups. Margaret, on occasion, has filled the breech – as have June and Gordon Brown of Essex, Ontario, and Marjorie and John Quinney of Strathroy, Ontario, and Alida Cook in Australia.

We gladly supply slides to any supporters willing to give presentations and are depending more and more on faithful supporters for such help.

Murray's team of travellers for 1984

During the war, I met a chap overseas, George P. Goodrow of Hamilton, Ontario. In the intervening almost forty years, he has been a friend and SCAW supporter, as well as assisting in our public relations.

In our slide presentations, we stress the positive, choosing to show the child *after* rather than *before*. I totally disagree with the shock approach of television documentaries. To me, they destroy the dignity of the child.

Songs, too, have been composed for SCAW. Two delightful ones were by Raymond Gould, of Islington, Ontario; another, a lovely lullaby by Bill Browne, a Jesuit Father from St. John's, Newfoundland; and a fourth by Bill Thacker, a long-time contributor from Sugar Grove, Ohio.

We are deeply indebted to all these people.

A little Tibetan refugee carries away his new kit

SUMMARY

1980, in particular, was quite a year. I was gone four months, travelling alone, during which time I was in four different countries (including Africa) in a five-day period.

In the remote outposts of the cold, wind-swept Himalayas, I spent nine nights in a tent. The bruises on these trips may be many, but the rewards are manifold.

Ben Benito of Kiwanis organized a fine and smooth distribution in the Philippines, using an air-conditioned mini-bus and processing 1000 children at 31 different locations. The year before (1983), in the Philippines, in one particular fast-paced day, 835 kits were distributed.

On the eve of our departure from Manila, where we had planned to supply a small number of kits but had found the need much greater, we announced a planned 1500 kits for the next year, and everyone was ecstatic!

In the Philippines, many say hello, grasp your hand and kiss it. In one area there, we were met by hundreds of children chanting "Long Live Canada" in Filipino and waving banners which read "Welcome SCAW, Ambassadors for Canada" and "Thank you, nice people of Canada."

What lies ahead? Our target for 1985-6 is 12 000 beds. With God's help, and the help of our marvellous supporters, we can and will reach this goal!

LETTERS FROM DISTRIBUTION CENTRES

"Two hundred families from Galas, Quezon City are grateful to you for the slumber kits they received. Most of these children come from the squatter areas of Quezon City and have never had any experience of wearing pajamas to bed. The following day, after the distribution, I visited one street and I saw many children in the street happily parading in their new, clean, and colorful pajamas. It was a sight to behold.

"The slumber kits have not only helped 200 children and their families but also provided additional and necessary income for at least 15 non-working mothers from our Home League Program, most of whom subsist on this income. The pillow cases and pajamas they sew are more durable, prettier and even cheaper than those being bought ready-made from our local markets.

"This project has helped me tremendously in my work as Corps Officer here at Quezon City. The children are now attending our Sunday School and outpost meetings regularly. The mothers are also coming to our weekly women's meeting. It opens up many opportunities for me in presenting the gospel of our Lord Jesus Christ. It also helped me with my public relations among the local leaders of our community."

From Captain R. MacKenzie writing about distributions in over eighteen Haitian centres in 1981:

". . . As the kits were loaded upon the shoulders of their new owners, a glow of pride and excitement radiated from each little one. When asked how little Marie would manage with this load, she responded by pointing

For one week we saved up all our "junk food" money and placed it in a plastic jar at school. We wanted to learn about the spirit of sharing and the real meaning behind Christmas. We talked about our own happy times and decided that a warm, snuggly bed was one of our favourite moments during the holidays. Cuddly new pyjamas was a treat we all enjoyed! After reading about your project we all agreed that we wanted our money to go to you. We hope that you will accept our small donation.

Our sincere thanks for the lovely pictures of the children who received our sleeping-kits last Christmas. It was such a thrill to place their pictures before our manger scene this year and watch the faces of our grandchildren as they presented their gifts. They were overjoyed to actually know where their gifts were going this year.

I received your pictures of the children receiving their little beds. I make my heart glad that I can make such a happy smile a a small in. When we have a bed to sleep in. When we have so much I am glad that I though Christ can help someone feel loved.

Herewith $25.00 being my fourth contribution to your very worthy cause.

The last time I won the office pool I sent the money to you and yesterday I was lucky to win again so here it is with enough to make up enough for 1 kit.

out that this was not a load but her very own "matla". So the stories go as almost 1000 children responded to the biggest treasure of their lives."

From Sister Christopher, Bombay, India:

" . . . We sisters had a marvellous time shopping for the materials and, women that we are, we enjoyed going around looking for the cheapest and best. To our good fortune, we were able to secure all the material we needed at government-controlled rates . . . . All the sewing was done by the sisters and by the elder girls themselves, with the result that our costs were cut to almost half, so we were able to buy extras such as a pair of towels each, even underwear and socks to wear to school and school uniforms . . . .

" . . . . I wish all the donors could see the children rolling on their bed-dings in sheer ecstasy. Thank you, and *may God, whom I picture chuckling*

MR. D. MURRAY DRYDEN
CHAMPION, WORLDS UNDERPRIVILEGED CHILDREN
DIRECTOR/FOUNDER SLEEPING CHILDREN AROUND THE WORLD

with contentment as He contemplates His children (Canadian and Indian united through these Slumber Kits), bless us all and unite us one day . . . ."

From Father Frank West in Darjeeling, India:
"The Slumber Kits have not only helped very positively in keeping 200 poor and needy Nepalese children and their families warm this winter (and this year our Darjeeling winter had been very cold, sometimes below freezing), but has also provided additional and necessary income for 24 poor mothers

from our *Functional Literacy Programme,* most of whom subsist on this income from stitching the comforters and the pyjamas . . . .

"The comforters, called "seraks" in Nepali, are made large (7' x 5') on purpose, for though the beneficiary was a single small child, the child would most naturally share the serak with the rest of the family. Probably it will be the warmest place in their single-room homes this winter, a winter which lasts from October to April."

BRIEF EXCERPTS FROM SUPPORTERS' LETTERS:

"I am so happy to have the pictures to see the happiness in their faces . . . ."

"It is true that those materials will be worn out as days go by, but the spirit of sharing will remain in their memories as they grow up and that there are people from other countries who care for them . . . ."

"I have been saving envelopes and I am mailing you a bundle. I hope you will put them to good use . . . ."

"Thank you for the letter and material. Hope you don't mind but I often photocopy the newsletters and pass them on to friends."

"In your letter to me you said you had a poster, "With God all things are possible." The Lord continues to show me how true this phrase is . . . . May God continue to bless your work and the children who receive the kits, but most of all, those who don't."

"Thank you for the beautiful photos of "Sleeping Children" you sent me. Just looking at the happy faces makes me feel good."

"We have some friends in Ottawa with a little daughter who will be two years old next August.

We had some plans to buy her a doll but the parents say that they would want her to share her good fortune with those who have less and that she has quite enough toys and clothes for the present.

Enclosed is our cheque dated *1 January 1984* to cover the cost of one kit for a child. While we would like to receive the receipt in due course, we would ask that the photo of "her" child go to the little girl. Her name and address are: _____"

Shortly after my return to Canada from Uganda, I had a letter from Dr. Elizabeth Hillman, Professor at the Janeway Child Health Centre in St. John's, Newfoundland. I am going to quote her, as it says it all and much better than I ever could:

"This past winter, I went to work in Uganda – chaotic, war-torn, post-Amin Uganda – and I thought of your programme when I worked on the children's ward in the hospital where; every night, there was looting. The mattresses were being stolen from under the sick and starving children. It was heartbreaking . . . .

A Sleeping Child

"Now I lay me down to sleep,"
I listened to my daughter's prayer,
"I pray the Lord my soul to keep" –
I gently stroked her soft blond hair.

A few more moments and I knew
She slept as every small child should,
Clean, warm and cozy, peaceful, too –
For her the world is bright and good.

I sat a short while longer there,
Then left and quietly closed the
    door;
And thought of children,
    everywhere,
Who that night slept on ground or
    floor.

I knew that somewhere in this world,
Millions of children had no beds,
They sleep with bodies cold and
    curled,
No soft pillows to lay their heads.

Why must a little girl or boy
Sleep in the way those children do,
While my daughter has warmth and
    joy –
With her own bed, and pillow, too?

When God designed earth, sky, and
    air,
Heaven's beauty in this world He
    styled –
But nothing fashioned can compare
With the face of a sleeping child.

If sleeping children round the World
Had beds the way our children do,
God's flag of love would be
    unfurled –
Their faces would show this beauty,
    too.

LORNE L. SMITH

"We have proposed that the children's ward be moved to a smaller, safer unit, and we are going back next year to help again. I wondered if you have ever offered beds to the children of Uganda, who have known nothing but war since, before, they were born in a country that was strong and proud and free – and will be so again. I have reliable contacts there – in Kampala – who have only the children's welfare at heart. I wonder if you would be interested in providing bedding for the children hospitalized in Old Mulago?"

"Our sincere thanks for the lovely pictures of the children who received our sleeping kits last Christmas. It was such a thrill to place their pictures before our manger scene this year and watch the faces of our grandchildren as they presented their gifts. They were overjoyed to actually know where their gifts were going this year."

"Herewith $25.00 being my fourth contribution to your very worthy cause.
"The last time I won the office pool I sent the money to you and yesterday I was lucky to win again so here it is with enough to make up enough for 1 kit."

NEWSPAPER CLIPPINGS
From *The Christian Science Monitor's* "Home & Family": (23 April 1984):
"Mr. Dryden, who says they can only begin to respond to the pleas for help pouring in from developing countries, states: 'It's like putting your finger in the dike. The need is so great.' "

From the 22 June 1972 *Etobicoke Guardian* article on our Retirement Dinner by Red Duddin:
"Father West, a Jesuit priest working with the Canadian Jesuits in Northern India spoke on Monday night of his first hand experiences in the area. 'I have seen tiny children sleeping on sidewalks, in the roadways and in the gutters. I have seen the fortunate ones that have received beds through the Sleeping Children Programme.' "

The Third World and Beyond

Working for five companies in the building materials business is a cinch compared to navigating in the cultural waters of 18 countries.

SEVEN WONDERS – PLUS

I often tell friends that heaven will have to be something really special – or I won't go, because I have already seen such wonderful sights in this world!

There were supposed to be Seven Wonders of the Ancient World, but I've discovered many more in my travels for SCAW. For a start:

Waterfalls   They just "grab" me! Four of the greatest must be our own Niagara Falls, the Iguassu Falls in Brazil, Victoria Falls on that hostile border between Zambia and Zimbabwe and the Gull Falls in Iceland. They are all spectacularly different.

Iguassu Falls, Brazil

Icebergs off Jakobshaven, Greenland

The Iguassu Falls, in the wilderness at the junction of Paraguay, Brazil and Argentina, are a sprawling, falling face of water higher than Niagara, and can be as wide as three miles across in the wet season. Actually, Iguassu is not one water-fall but 21 cataracts formed by the many rivers which join here, and they're each as different as their names – Devil's Throat, Three Musketeers, Bosetti . . . . It is only from the air that the full spectacle hits the viewer, though to stand close by the falls is to feel the earth trembling along with the water's thunder.

Thousands of miles away, on another continent, the water of the Victoria Falls hurtles through a high, narrow chasm on the Zambezi River, to drop 400 feet in a series of "diaphanous veils of water". I was told that the roar and towering spray can be detected 25 miles away. My two-hour boat tour on the Zambezi included tea and cookies served outdoors.

Icebergs   I'm a nut for icebergs! The "deep-freeze centre" for the world's icebergs is a tiny settlement in Greenland called Jakobshaven, which can be reached only by boat or helicopter. Here one finds 450 Danes, 2900 Greenlanders – and about 6000 sledge dogs.

The icebergs, in incredible shapes and colours, appear majestic across the water – like a dazzling fleet, as they seem to ride at anchor in the harbour and the water beyond, as far as the eye can see. As I watched – totally fascinated – for hours from my hotel window, I felt that I was witnessing an international play-by-play chess match, the icebergs moving ever so slowly this way and that. Those icebergs were a sight which I often recall with awe.

Pyramids of Gizeh   It may seem trite to inlcude these pyramids among my outstanding travel experiences, but anyone who has seen them – and the Sphinx – knows they cannot justly be left out. My favourite time at the pyramids was late afternoon, with the sun setting behind these massive antiquities, but seen at any time they are unforgettable by reason of their sheer mass. They are an overwhelming human achievement, and their aloof and melancholy serenity – even now when a four-lane highway runs almost to the foot of the Great Pyramid – is awesome. Even the sand around the pyramids amazed me . . . . it is as fine as face powder.

Our tour guide – an unshaven, toothless chainsmoker – gave the ancient Greeks and Romans "hell" all day, describing them as grave robbers and murderers, and doing so with such venom that we felt it had all just happened. He also informed us that King Rameses II had 40 wives, 65 children, and had lived 125 years – whereas his son, when he became king, took one wife only and lived a mere 18 years.

Countries   As to favourite countries, if I had to choose only one to visit, it would be *India*. To me, no other has so much to offer as far as scenery . . . . It is one continuous panorama.

India seems to be stitched together by its trains; the railway stations seethe with people, many of whom have no ticket, it seems, and no hope of getting on a train.

One time, right in the middle of all these constantly moving people, I spotted a small boy, about 5, lying asleep on the stone floor. He was totally alone; people just stepped around him and no one seemed concerned.

India is one place in my travels where I have never felt afraid to walk the streets at night or to venture alone into villages and markets. There's something innately peaceable in the people, which is why I suppose passive resistance organized by Gandhi against the British was so successful.

Hawaii is of course, a favourite with most travellers. I met Margaret at Honolulu in the Aloha fashion with a "lei" and an embrace. I had just flown in from Tokyo, and Margaret from Vancouver. No people is possibly more mixed than the Hawaiian, and Margaret made the statement that if she belonged to a minority race, she would prefer to live in Hawaii. The people seem to get along beautifully together. We were amazed to learn that the beautiful sandy beaches and construction depend on sand being brought in regularly (from Australia, mainly).

And I have cities among my special memories:

Moscow, at the time of the Soviet/Canada 1972 hockey series, holds special memories for me. I recall four Bostonians who whipped out typed cards bearing the words of *O Canada* and their enthusiasm in singing along with us. And I will never forget the spontaneous rendering of *We Wish You a Merry Christmas* by 3000 Canadians, in one great swelling voice, when arriving in the arena lobby from rinkside to find a blinding snowstorm raging outside . . . .

My first impression of Moscow, back in 1967, was that – except for a few vehicles – there were thousands and thousands of people walking, walking . . . all wearing the same dark clothing, and the women the monotonous fur hats. This, of course, has changed.

Warsaw I remember for a charming and unexpected adventure. I had booked a sightseeing tour of the city that wintry morning and was the only one on the bus until we arrived at another hotel and picked up 70 young students from Bucknell University in Pennsylvania. They were on a 3½ week tour of Eastern Europe. What a courteous, bright-eyed bunch of 18-22 year olds! They "adopted" me and took turns sitting next to me so we could get acquainted. This was their first big trip and there was a wonderful enthusiasm about them and a touching innocence. They were better American ambassadors than any number of politicians.

Copenhagen is one of the liveliest cities in Europe – mainly because of the Tivoli Gardens. From May to September, Tivoli is a wonderland of lakes, flowers, fireworks, and illuminated fountains in the heart of the city. Under a full moon, the Gardens seem enchanted, and there is something to please every taste – symphony concerts, open-air dances, a midway, pantomime, international variety acts, marching bands. . . .

Murray travelling the hard way in Greece, 1967

Singingapore is another very special city. It's an amazing demonstration of how a unique mixture of people and religions can live together in peace and prosperity. It's also the cleanest, most efficient, most corruption-free country in south-east Asia. As well, it is probably one of the few places where cabbies are trilingual. Most of them speak Malay (the official language), English and their own family language.

Chinese, Indians, Malays, Indonesians and a dozen racial permutations live harmoniously in Singapore, the world's third largest port. Here the schoolchildren wear immaculate white and blue uniforms. This is where young Stamford Raffles, of the East India Company, founded a trading post in 1819. I think he'd be proud of Singapore today. I know that I love it.

In *Tokyo* I have been fortunate to receive several meal invitations to private homes. Dining, Japanese-style, is a delight. Tours of the city are conducted by guides who are well trained and brimful of personality. On some tours, a commercial photographer takes a group picture of the bus party at the first stop and furnishes a souvenir postcard to each sightseer at the conclusion of the trip.

In spite of the fact that 97% of all Japan's gasoline is imported, it has one of the lowest taxi rates. The drivers dress and drive like cowboys but wear gloves of impeccable white. Owing to the high price of heating fuel, and to show their practicability, the Japanese freeze their huge Olympic swimming pool in winter to enable hundreds of skaters to enjoy its facilities.

Perth, West Australia is a special favourite. With a modest population of 750 000, it possesses all the charm and cultural advantages of a metropolis, but is almost devoid of the many inconveniences one encounters in those "populous nightmares".

I think a great deal of Perth's beauty comes from the skilful use, in most of their buildings, of brick in a wide range of colours peculiar to the clay and shale deposits of that region – but then I am prejudiced by my interest in building materials!

Travel is thrilling only when there still is mystery . . . when what is around the corner is unknown.

ESCAPADES

Denmark – "Meet the Danes" Programme The year we started Sleeping Children Around the World, I took a side trip to Denmark for a few days and decided to participate in their "Meet the Danes" programme. And meet the Danes I did – one in particular!

I got a room in a private home and was assured I would be welcome, even though it was almost midnight. I bought some fruit and took a taxi to the home of Mrs. Fratz, where I had to climb three steep flights of stairs with all my luggage.

Mrs. Fratz was a friendly, grey-haired widow who spoke some English. She seemed pleased to meet a Canadian. We shared my fruit and a bottle of her tonic water and talked for an hour. The next morning she wakened me with a tray of

Murray at a Greek theatre-in-the-round in 1967

coffee and biscuits. As I left, I handed her a package of cigarettes which someone had given me. "I hope you don't smoke, but maybe you can give them to somebody," I told her. "I don't smoke, that's why I'm so healthy!", I added.

Mrs. Fratz smiled, "I do smoke, but I am healthy too!", and she did a bit of chest thumping – then motioned me towards her bedroom. I followed her reluctantly, wondering what she had in mind. Inside, across the doorjamb, was a chrome bar. She grabbed it, chinned herself nine times, and then stood back, looking a bit smug.

I took over, and did 20 chinups – just to show the flag and restore my masculine superiority. She laughed and said, "Good, but I am . . . ." Here she looked coy, then proceeded to outline the number 67 on the door.

This is one of the delightful things that can never happen at a Hilton or a Sheraton. . . .

Portugal — Tea at the Palace   In February, 1980, I was making a bed distribution in Portugal and, through the Salvation Army, I was tendered an invitation by the wife of President Manuelo (Eaves).

We had distributed 300 beds just outside Lisbon that day and photographed the children in their beds. I had not taken time to eat and was hungry when I got back to my hotel.

I climbed into my best togs, but could not appease my hunger until "dinnah" which is served after eight in Portugal. So, I decided to grab something en route. However, I could not bring myself to eating in the establishments I entered, so decided to settle for a bottle of milk and drink it in the taxi on the way to the Presidential Palace. The clerk put the bottle in a brown paper bag, and I went out to catch a taxi.

It was almost 6 p.m. and everyone was heading home from their places of employment, resulting in every taxi being engaged. Time was slipping by, and my date with Maria Manuela was for 7 o'clock. I began to panic as it appeared that I was about to "scupper" the chance of a lifetime.

I enlisted help from the shopkeepers, who had no better luck. They told me that my only chance would be by bus; when I saw how jammed they all were, this seemed futile, too. However, I was given the magic number and I queued, getting my one foot on the step as the driver was about to close the door, but managing to get in.

Two ladies standing by the driver translated as they asked me where I was going. When I told them I had a 7-o'clock appointment with Maria Manuela at Belang Palace, they looked at me disbelievingly. One remarked: "Are you going to drink milk with the president's wife?" The brown paper had worn away, disclosing the gilt cap of my milk bottle, and there was just no mistaking that it was a bottle of milk!

When I told the whole story, the women were on my side and kept imploring the driver to drive faster and to close the doors more quickly. It was up and down dale as the bus lurched through those narrow streets. They also told me I should drink the milk, so I pulled the cap and, every time the bus stopped, I

Workers cleaning hemp in an Indian village

Caged girls in a red light district of Bombay, India

tipped the bottle up and took a swallow, always watching that I didn't dribble on my navy blue outfit. Finally, just as I took the last swig, the driver pointed and called, "The Palace!"

Guards, at 7 p.m. sharp, led me inside and then, a few minutes later, I was ushered into a beautiful room where I met Maria. What a thrill it was talking to this pretty and gracious woman while enjoying tea and cakes! She emphasized that she wanted, through me, to express her thanks to all SCAW donors for their help to her children. It was a high point of the 1980 trip, but I still break into a cold sweat every time I think of how close I came to "blowing" it.

Uganda: Close call!   In 1981, we undertook to distribute 500 Slumber Kits to Uganda. Working through the Salvation Army headquarters in Nairobi, the necessary materials were purchased and made up in Kenya, then shipped by lorry to Tororo. The required materials were unavailable in Uganda at any price.

We spent a hectic week distributing the units in nine different small rural regions. Former President Idi Amin had taken from the farmers great quantities of coffee, tobacco and cotton, exported them and been paid for them, but did not pay the farmers. Consequently, they refused to grow further crops. Black Market had taken over . . . bread was $6 a loaf, soap $5 a cake and pineapples $20 a head. Violence was everywhere.

Near the Salvation Army headquarters in Kampala, a few minutes before I arrived, a woman was washing her clothes when a soldier came up and, with no warning, he shot her and took the cake of soap. There were at least a dozen other similar incidents during the week I was in the country.

On our last day, we had trouble with our small station wagon as we travelled from Tororo to Kampala. We distributed a quantity of Slumber Kits en route, but a tire puncture (the patch alone cost us $10) put us in darkness. At each road block, we had trouble with the military as, in every instance, they asked for some of the supplies we were carrying in the vehicle. Each time, we had to make a decision whether to give in or not. In some cases, inflexibility would have been disastrous. We finally decided that, at future barriers, we would not put on the light inside the vehicle, thereby eliminating the temptation.

Outside Kampala, we passed what looked like a potted plant on the road and, when Major Baywaters did not stop, I reminded her of some other queer-looking barriers, so she decided to reverse. Lucky for us that she did because, in a few seconds, two soldiers appeared out of the dark and cleared us through. A couple of miles further on, we approached a large branch in the middle of the road. Although it looked like the work of a windstorm, we decided to stop. Again it proved to be a check-point, as a huge soldier in camouflage appeared out of the darkness with an automatic pointed at us. He reeked of alcohol. The Major carried on a conversation in Swahili for some time, and suddenly the inside of the car lit up. He signalled us through. I was baffled.

Afterwards, the trembling Major, a 62-year-old Australian, interpreted the conversation. The soldier had said, "You have a guerilla beside you, and I am going to shoot him." The Major replied, "No, he is not a guerilla, but a man from

Murray, the shutterbug, in Manila, Philippines

Canada." Again he repeated his threat. Then he instructed Stella, "I want you to put out the headlights and to tell him to get out of the vehicle." At that point, she said, "Lord help me! Tell me what to do." Almost instantly, she eased open the car door, triggering the inside light. A glance, and he signalled us through.

Tanzania – Monkeys and Elephants!   One of the most unexpected incidents I ever encountered was in Tanzania. I arrived at the Hotel Manyara after having spent several days on a photographic safari. It had been a thrilling trip, but now I was tired and dirty and looking forward to a good sleep in a real room, instead of a tent, and a long soak in a real tub. (Monkeys had been jumping around on the roof of my tent the previous night.)

I could hardly wait to get into the bathroom but, when I did, I found – to my stupefaction – there wasn't even a dribble of water, hot or cold. I couldn't get a reply on the house phone, so I raced downstairs, arriving at the same time as the other unwashed members of our safari party.

"Sorry, sir," the desk clerk said, without batting an eyelid, "an elephant stepped on our water line this morning and broke it."

Teheran after midnight   Unhappy with my hotel in Teheran one night, I told the desk clerk I was going somewhere else. He pleaded with me; then the manager came out and offered me a drink, but I phoned the downtown Elizabeth Hotel and found a room available at $17.

By this time of night, out in the "boondocks" of Teheran, taxis were difficult to find. Several which did arrive had drivers who looked as if they'd just been cut down from the gallows. I waved them on, finally accepting one whose driver looked reasonable, but there was very little on the vehicle to denote that it was a taxi.

We'd only been a short distance when he stopped and picked up another man, obviously a friend, who looked equally disreputable. They sat together in the front whispering and looking back at me. As the drive lengthened, and we didn't seem to be any closer to the city, I wondered if I was being taken out into the desert to be bumped off. . . . Finally, to my relief, the city lights began to get brighter and the driver pulled up in front of the hotel. He refused to let me have my luggage, however, until I had put the fare safely into his hand. Obviously the furtive conversation which I had thought so sinister was about my willingness or ability to pay the tab.

Nepal-Himalayan "Assault"   My ten days in the Himalayas in 1981 were an adventure I will not soon forget.

Twenty-six porters had begun, on January 5th, to move 1000 beds (approximately 10 tons) into position to be taken up into four villages never before serviced by SCAW. Leaving Katmandu at 0800 on January 18th, little did I know what lay ahead. . . .

After a mere continental breakfast at the Shanker Hotel, we set forth on our day's journey. I was still wearing my usual heavy walking shoes, which caused me

Distribution of kits in Uganda

Sidewalk barbershop in Lahore, Pakistan

to slide a lot as we began our ascent. After an hour out, I switched over to a pair of running shoes, and fared much better.

Up to the third hour, the terrain was no worse nor better than I had expected – a few treacherous spots, particularly alongside a deep and fast-running river. We had 3 porters, a guide and a cook and we stopped for 5 minutes every 30 minutes. The cook was anxious to ply me with tea.

After sailing along for four hours, word came to halt for light refreshments. I was to know, later, that this was the notice of a formidable "enemy" lying ahead. At 1630 we were given the order to "attack". It was up, up, up on narrow and slippery trails, and it was getting darker. Earlier, our trip routing had been changed from a 3-hour to a 6-hour objective. I sensed that the game was to kill me off early. My confidence was indeed gradually being shot down – I was even thinking of the possibility of an air lift! The thought of 9 more days of this torture almost made me sick.

We finally reached camp at dark, and a small party welcomed us with suitable garlands and gifts of eggs and wee bananas. I was on the receiving end of some 23 eggs in that one day!

A fine red nylon tent was set up; it was to be my home for 9 nights. The cook promised me a feast, and indeed I was ready for it. After that last leg up "Heartbreak Mountain", my 0730 continental breakfast had long gone. When my feast arrived, the rice was cold, but I ate it. However, the bits and pieces purported to be chicken were laced with spices, so I had to pass them on to one of the porters. I did enjoy a bowl of soup with chopped onion tops, though, and the canned pineapple slices, the juice of which I had sipped from the punctured tin at the last rest stop. As to the food the rest of the way, it was grim!

Retiring time was usually around 2000 hours, but I was anxious to see a few homes and how the children normally slept. So, around 2130, we visited 3 houses and took photographs of the sleeping children. (The following night, we retraced our steps and took shots of the same kiddies in their new slumber kits.) When, later, I stretched out in the tent, I could not believe the hardness of my bed. Underneath my oriental-size sleeping bag was a ⅜" thick piece of heavy rubber, 30" wide, and this was supported by – the ground! The mattress looked like plywood and it was just as soft! I slept poorly, with all my regular clothes on, plus my Nepal hat.

With reveille around 0530, on day #2 I rose at six chimes. After instant oatmeal for breakfast and some tea, we went over to Krishna's house, where the sleeping kits were stored for that particular village of Kunuwal.

The sum of $25 280, Canadian had been sent to Katmandu in October and administered through Mr. Michael Rojik, Assistant Manager, Toronto Camera Centre, who, for the past few years, had been responsible for the construction of 17 primary schools in Nepal. Being thorough, businesslike, honest and a stickler for details, it was a pleasure to deal with Mr. Rojik.

Safe storage was a problem, but everything was intact upon our arrival for distribution. In three of the locations, this was done from schools, and with one exception – when it rained – the photographing of the kiddies in their beds was done outside. This was ideal, as there was so much space for the families to gather, and this furnished a splendid Nepalese background for our pictures. One of the classrooms became the pyjama change room. After the photograph was taken, the child's parent was handed the donor's label; then he or she presented it at the stock room, where the balance of items was issued.

We found that, in many areas, pyjamas are not worn to bed, and this new sleeping attire became their best dress. It was amusing to later spot the children dotting the mountainside as we trekked between villages. Bless their little hearts, those pj's were an exciting relief from their tatters and rags – and all for the cost of around two bucks.

The trek to the second village, Mathillchap, was a real killer. The day was warm and the slopes steep, with many of the pathways strewn with large, loose broken stone. At a couple of waterfalls, I trotted out my little filter, then quaffed the cool goodness. At the school site, the porters set up my tent *in a classroom, where the floors were mud and the stakes went in easily.*

Getting to the third village, Bhorjyang, was a "breeze" – less than three hours over less-than-exhausting terrain. However, travelling from there to Chukka was something else. We left at ten minutes to seven, with several of the villagers accompanying us. I think this is a beautiful custom – not just a wave from a Canadian front door, nor that of a Korean seeing you to the gate.

After a gruelling five hours, it was time for a top strategy meeting. Our objective, Chukka, was still 3 hours away. I winced! Besides being hard on my feet, the ol' stomach was giving me some trouble. It was decided to make a one-hour *descent* to a possible camp site. This route was a precarious one, but we finally landed at the site – a house, where 3 days earlier, we had taken care of 8 of the children under 11 years, and all 8 were sporting their new attire.

As soon as the tent was pitched, I flopped on the hard rubber and, in spite of 10 kids, roosters, goats, water buffalo, dogs, etc., I was "out" for 2 hours.

On this particular morning, January 24th, I pulled myself out of the sleeping bag at 0515 and, on exiting, I tripped over one of the tent stakes, causing me to pitch head-first over a 10-ft parapet stone wall in the total dark! My glasses flew off, also my watch, and I picked myself up out of a field of rape in flower, a field that was also littered with large stones. One shoe and the flashlight had left me as I plunged, but my spectacles and watch were OK and I could not believe that I had only a barked knee and arm.

The group had slept through it all. As there was no way I could find my way to the upper level, I had to call the guides. They, too, could not believe that I was not injured. And to think it happened 17 trekking hours from any kind of road where help might be found. There was certainly no doubt that *He* was looking after me.

The rest of the trip to Chukka was not too tough, and the following morning we distributed 100 beds before it began to rain, at which time we had to move inside to give out the remaining 150, completing over 1000 for Nepal.

The children, "face-wise", look healthy – it is only when you see their bodies and the distended bellies that you are hit with the truth. Many could not fasten

Malnutrition is a big belly in Haiti or anywhere.

the third button on their pyjama tops. (A larger size will have to be considered another time.)

Back at the Shanker Hotel in Katmandu, it was a shave, haircut, and the bathtub — but not necessarily in that order!

Darjeeling, India that breath-taking scenery. . . I've made eleven trips to Darjeeling, which is a lovely town perched on the edge of the Himalayas, and each time I promised myself that it was the last.

At Bagdogra, which is the nearest airport for Darjeeling, for some mystic reason there are few taxi drivers at the airport. You have to get a bus to the bus depot and hire a rickshaw to take you into Silguri – all the while humping your luggage along – where you may be able to rent a taxi for the four-hour drive to Darjeeling.

The road to Darjeeling is, of course, not lighted. It is paved in a half-hearted way, and about the width of a trail, and is embellished with deep, plunging gorges and with potholes the size of elephant traps. It is also uphill all the way, with dizzying precipitous drops on either side of the unfenced road.

On one trip, in 1972, I wasn't really surprised when the right rear wheel flew off our taxi after the first hour. A call for help was sent to the next village by another taxi driver, and a rescue truck with a mechanic arrived about an hour later. It took him two hours to fix the wheel. We started off again but now it was almost dark and a heavy fog had descended, cutting visibility to just a few feet in front of the single dim headlight. To add to the driver's task, a road-mending truck had dropped piles of gravel in the middle of the road (probably weeks before), often around a sharp corner, and several times he managed to stop with the radiator nuzzling the pile. After a couple of narrow misses, the chickens who were swaying on top of the taxi became hysterical and clucked piteously the rest of the way. I kept saying my prayers, mentally making my will, and wondering about the cost of shipping my body back home. . . .

We finally reached Darjeeling after midnight. I was almost too numb to move, paralyzed by fright and fatigue. I remember fervently clasping the driver's hand, thanking him, and giving him an exorbitant tip when he dropped me outside the Windamere Hotel. Actually, he had to drop us at the bottom of a steep path because Darjeeling is more hilly than San Francisco and the Windamere is perched a hundred feet up on the hillside.

But – my ordeal wasn't over! On this trip, 200 slumber kits had been distributed by the Canadian Jesuit Fathers to various one-room hovels and lean-tos that clung to the side of the mountains. Because I insisted on getting photos of the children after they were asleep, I had to pick my way, accompanied by two students carrying lanterns, up and down the slopes in the dark, often stepping on dogs and pigs, or frightening chickens. When I saw, the next morning, where I'd been climbing in the dark, I couldn't believe it. (After this experience, I decided that we didn't have to wait for the children to be asleep and I took photos on subsequent trips at the Jesuits' Hayden Hall during the day.)

I had thought conditions in the cities and in the hot, dirty plains were dreadful, but here, in the midst of breathtaking scenery, it was just as bad. Children lived and slept in holes under roads, in sewage pipes, or in one-room shacks where a common bed of boards and sacking had to be shared by seven or eight family members.

One of the workers in the mission wrote to me later saying, "I see the effect of your gifts even in the daytime. On several occasions, when visiting the homes of children in our Mother and Child Care programme, I have to sit and smile encouragingly as a proud mother shows the way she cares for the new bright pillowcase and bedsheets. For many of our half-naked toddlers, the bright yellow, blue or red flannel pyjamas have quickly become their best outfits. Not only do they sleep comfortably and fashionably in them, but they also appear in them at functions, or when marketing or attending our day care centre for malnourished children."

In early February of 1972, when I was staying at the Windamere Hotel, I had five heavy blankets on my bed and two hot water bottles. At breakfast, I was mildly whining about the discomfort and feeling rather forlorn and far from home there on the icy "Roof of the World". That same night, a friend took me to an orphanage that I'd said I wanted to see.

Several hundred children were lying like cordwood on the bare floor in their thin daytime clothes, a ragged blanket shared by every two or three children. (Even so, they were incomparably luckier than thousands outside, some of whom were lying in lean-tos made of flattened kerosene cans on the mountainside. Against my wishes, some of the children were wakened (it was almost midnight)

During India trip with Mitka, frequent car problems were encountered on the mountain roads.

to sing a couple of songs for me, their breath rising like steam from their little mouths. I went back to the Windamere and my five thick blankets, thoroughly ashamed of myself.

You can believe the Windamere's brochure which advertises "rooms with view", because the hotel looks towards majestic Everest, 100 miles away, towering above all the snow-covered mountain ranges in between. The air is dazzling and everything sparkles. I got up about 4 a.m. one morning to see the sunrise flood the mountains with colour at Tiger Hill.

Early each day, twelve beggars take their position on the path leading up to the hotel – six on the way up and six on the way down. It's a profitable "beat"; I noticed that the guests, who were mainly wealthy Indians, made a point of dropping something in each bowl as they emerged from the hotel every day. In slack periods, the beggars, some horribly crippled, one a woman with a child at her breast (not necessarily her own since some rent them for better effect), would look for lice in each other's hair. I was irresistibly reminded of seeing monkeys in zoos doing the same thing. Begging is alien and degrading to us, but it's an acceptable occupation in the East. If they weren't allowed to beg, they would die. There is no welfare system to look after the poor.

A Muslim gives alms for credit or merit, and most beggars believe they are helping you on your way to Heaven by allowing you to give to them. I find it helps to say "Moph Koro" (Forgive me). This means you are asking his forgiveness because you are unable to give. Upon hearing this, most beggars will leave, unless they are very persistent.

That Kalimpong Ropeway!　1982: Over two rivers, some 600 feet below, in an *open* carriage – for 1¼ miles – I found myself wondering how old that rope bridge was. Instead of admitting to my two companions that I was in trouble and afraid of being pronounced a coward, I gazed at the dark heavens and prayed, thus avoiding my earlier almost-fatal glance *down*. It was a ride I would not choose to repeat, thank you!

The Road to Mahabaleshwar　Using a battered 1964 Ambassador, we called for a passenger, Mr. Mitha, at the mosque. I felt my first twinge of anxiety when Mr. Mitha explained that he had felt he should pray for the safety and success of our journey and his friends nodded gravely. Little did I realize that it would take 16 hours and the combined benevolence of Krishna, Allah and Jehovah to get us over those miles, full of potholes, to Bombay.

The narrow, poorly paved road, full of potholes, wound steadily up into the mountains and it was not long before we ran into a road block in the 100° temperature. Radiators boiled over, motors seized up and women in saris helped push cars off to the side. We finally got going again but had to keep stopping for goats and cattle and to fill the radiator, at which time Mr. Mitha would get out, go down on his knees on his prayer mat beside the road and, facing Mecca, would bow in prayer. At sunset we had to make a special stop for prayers.

It was nearly 3 a.m. as we drove into a sleeping Bombay, its streets and sidewalks strewn with thousands of bodies wrapped in rags and sacks — temporarily released from the hungry reality of their waking lives.

The Monsoons   Leaving Bandung, Java, in 1982, in a loaded minibus, we were caught en route by a monsoon rain as we drove through the mountains, encountering washouts, landslides and typhoon gales. My exclamations of "O brother!" and "Holy Cow!" – as we hit craters in the road – must have been heard for some distance. Finally we reached our stopping point at 3 a.m. As I crawled under the mosquito net, a local cockerel crowed three times only and I was reminded of Peter. I was just getting to sleep at 4 a.m. when the Muslims began chanting their morning prayers. Believe you me, we went to bed with the hens after that day's distribution of 500 beds.

The Road to Kulawi   When I journeyed to the Celebes, Indonesia, half a world away, for the first time in 1978, I found this country to be a beautiful chain of islands, with green mountains and Eden-like scenery, and with sparkling clean air and unpolluted rivers. But, sadly, there is poverty there too. . . .

When we set out from Palu in a Land Rover along the cart tracks, which pass for roads outside the few towns, we found that many bridges over small rivers had been washed out, and we had to drive through water which often came up to the running-boards. I kept my eyes glued to the gorgeous scenery and assumed, optimistically, that the driver knew what he was doing. It took us over three hours to reach Kulawi – less than 40 miles from Palu, which means that we averaged about 12 mph. I had thought the roads in India were the world's worst – until the Celebes!

Staying at the Salvation Army compound (which included a school and a small hospital) with Captain and Mrs. Tondi, I had a small, spotless room with a mosquito net over the bed and a kerosene lantern on the floor, which gave me a comfortable feeling all night.

People in this part of Indonesia keep geese, chicken and ducks, as well as one or more dogs, so there is no lack of noise through the night. The rooster chorus starts before dawn – about 3 a.m. I was up at 6 a.m. the first morning there, but the staff had been up and working for some time in their starched whites.

The Tondi sons, aged 8 and 10, were up too, washing themselves in the spring water piped into the compound through large bamboo pipes. After that, it was the children's job to feed all the animals, including a pet parrot. At breakfast, grace was sung in Indonesian and, after the meal, someone gave a five-minute devotion.

At Gimpu, which is a clearing in the jungle, the excited children and their parents were waiting for us at a small Salvation Army church under towering cocoanut palms. The pews were constructed of three long bamboo poles fastened together to form rigid seats without backs. I just hoped the services were kept mercifully short!

Tokyo, Palm Sunday – and Hockey!   Palm Sunday is my favourite Sunday of the whole year. I revel in its triumphant message. In April, 1976, I enjoyed a long

Grand Hotel, Taipei, Taiwan

walk through the blossoming avenues of Tokyo to a Lutheran church. Later, I boarded a Canadian Pacific flight, which landed in Vancouver the same afternoon. I checked into a hotel and discovered that the Montreal Canadiens and Ken, our son, were playing in the Stanley Cup playoffs that afternoon, which I was able to enjoy via television.

Later, I attended a thrilling service with four combined choirs in a beautiful Baptist church. Two services on Palm Sunday on different sides of the world, and a hockey game from the other end of the country – all on the same day!

Physically or mentally handicapped in Developing Countries – If it's hard to be poor in the developing countries, it's unbearable to be physically or mentally handicapped as well. There isn't the money to even support the fit, and the fit can barely survive – let alone those who have health problems along with their poverty. Many children are retarded because of malnutrition. If it were not for homes run by various foreign churches and organizations, many of these helpless children would be utterly abandoned by everyone. Desperate parents beg these homes to take at least one more child, but there is never enough space to meet the need.

At the Salvation Army's Joytown Crippled Centre and The Blind School in Thika, Kenya, the blind children refer to the crippled children as "tractors" because of all their metal. They, in turn, call the blind children "trains" because they move around holding on to one another's shoulders – and both groups are sorry for the other's handicap.

Distribution at
Salvation Army Blind School,
Thika, Kenya, 1972

From our 1982 Newsletter: Following a 325-bed distribution with the Chembur Rotarians, about fifteen of us went back to the orphanage around midnight. The 325 retarded kiddies, although in barrack-room style accommodation, looked so angelic and loved as they slept in their new beds. But next door it was difficult to choke back the tears as we gazed on the unlucky. They looked as though no one cared a damn. . . . It is not fair. They too have souls.

From our 1983 Newsletter   Calcutta – Boys' Town – After bedding down 174 boys there, they began calling us "Uncle". Never have we had so many nephews. Father Bob D'Souza explained that not one of the boys had a single relative. Their insecurity is pathetic. Father Bob is caught in a dilemma for he had a long list of homeless younger boys off the street for whom he had no room and yet he could not cut the older boys adrift for fear of what could happen to them. It was clear that they dreaded the day when they might be forced to leave their "brothers".

Surfers Paradise in Australia

The People   There are so many beautiful people . . . so many who have touched my life, never knowing how much they've given me. . . .

I think of courteous black Masri, in the Poste Restante cage at Medan Post Office in Sumatra, his beaming smile lighting up his face like a Christmas tree; Mastri always seemed more sad than I was when there was no mail waiting for me . . . the Stockholm bus driver who gave me my first taxi ride – in a bus! I was to visit friends in a suburb, 25 miles out, for dinner and I had just missed the bus by one minute. The next bus was already at the bus station but not due to leave for an hour. The driver told me to get in and he drove me 15 miles to a main intersection, then flagged down a private car, which dropped me at my hosts' door . . . .

. . . and I think, too, of those wonderful Bombay taxi drivers – one, especially – a little man who looked about 90 years old and who wore thick pebble glasses. He was tough-looking, but could he drive! Time after time, he got us out of what seemed to be inevitable multiple crashes with bullock carts, trucks, rickshaws, etc. (while I built up a real stockpile of fervent prayers).

And when I think of Calcutta, I think of Das, the shoeshine boy, who works just outside the entrance of the Great Eastern Hotel. Skinny, ragged and no doubt hungry most of the time, his face lights up like a forest fire when he smiles. In a city where most people go barefoot, and where those who do wear shoes realize the futility of having anything cleaned in filthy Calcutta, the shoeshine boy's business isn't exactly flourishing, but Das always grins and my resistance crumbles. And, if I can't use his services, he always says cheerfully, "Next time, sir?"

It's meeting people like this on my travels that keeps me going. . . .

Some of the finest people I have met both here and abroad are those who listen to the *pain of the world* – and *do* something about it. Often these people spend their lives in self-imposed exile, where the need is greatest, and what is their reward? – not much compared to the sums we pay our hockey players, our entertainers, our politicians.

The radiance of the human spirit shines in a dark world. . . .

CHAPTER THIRTEEN

Travel Abroad

Visas   A recent appointee, Multiculturalism Minister David Collenette, immediately announced that he was seriously considering Visa requirements for visitors from most countries. The announcement knocked the breath out of those of us who are involved with this industry. Imagine the chaos if these countries were to adopt retaliatory measures. Visualize, too, the unnecessarily tedious, expensive and hazardous exercise of obtaining visas for, say, half a dozen countries. (As of August 1984, the Indian Government requires a visa.) Your passport could conceivably be passed around embassies in Ottawa, Montreal, New York, etc. Eventually, in all likelihood Canada Post would end up losing it!

CIDA (Canadian International Development Agency)   It is my contention that CIDA does not adequately monitor its generous contributions to the Developing Countries. Too, I feel that there are too many chiefs in Hull and too few Indians out in the field. We are told that CIDA depends largely on the numerous agencies which it funds to oversee the disbursement of these tax dollars. One of the weaknesses here is that these agencies are frequently at the mercy of the corrupt local governments. Too often, they are forced into a compromise position in order to get their visas extended. There are many agencies – 52 in Bangladesh alone, at last count – and most are anxious to stay.

Foreign Banks   Canada desperately needs more foreign banks. For several years, I transferred money via the simple bank draft. It was inexpensive but undependable. Often the bank at the other end would not cash it, necessitating its coming back to Canada for confirmation. It was ponderously slow, often frustrating our cooperative agency for as many as six weeks. This meant that the kits were not ready upon my arrival.

Three years ago, my bank manager suggested that I send the money by wire, assuring me it would be faster and safer. While it may be safer, and more expensive, it has not been faster. As a matter of fact, this departure has, on several occasions, tied our operation into knots, resulting in my arriving in the country for distribution only to discover that the agency had not received the money. Result: postponement of the programme, disappointed donors, needless tracing costs, post mortems upon arrival back in Canada and, always, the inevitable "buck passing". Canadian banks blame it on the foreign bank, and vice versa. After all the "sweat and tears" expended to raise the money, only to have the banking industry louse us up is inexcusable. I have suffered too long at their hands and now feel the need, with many others, for the entry of Third World foreign banks into this country.

Travel Language An international travel language is something I've been yammering about for years. With more and more people travelling all the time, it has become urgent. A simple 1000-word vocabulary in possibly twenty of the world's most used languages, would be a good start. Grammar would be skipped and an inexpensive travel dictionary issued. Business on both continents which cater to the travelling public could see that their personnel had a good working knowledge of this "Travtalk". Surely this is a project that the Association of Travel Agents or the United Nations might get behind.

International Telephone Calls When every country is eager to attract foreign exchange, I am amazed at the manner in which many of them handle international telephone calls. Book a call to Canada from the Calcutta exchange and you will usually wait at least four hours!

When you get inside the cramped booth, the door will not close properly, jeopardizing the quiet needed for hearing. And there is absolutely no table or ledge on which to lay your note pad. Have you ever tried writing uphill with a ballpoint pen and your pad against a wall? At $4 a minute, one such experience is enough! But what a joy to make a similar call from Oslo, where the telephone exchange provides a large, almost soundproof room – complete with a table and chair.

International Mail When posting mail in many foreign countries, it is advisable to observe the clerk rubber-stamp your postage. Incidentally, it is not unusual to receive mail with the corner of the envelope torn off. (Just peeking. . . !)

Canadian Newspapers Overseas When away from home for an extended period, I almost die to see a Canadian newspaper! The Embassy Reading Rooms offer papers one to two months old – an insult for Canadians, considering how our government wastes money. I would suggest that, instead of stocking archive material only, they consider furnishing Air Mail copies of one leading daily provincial paper, and then change provinces each month. In Bucharest, the Inter-Continental Hotel rents a copy of the N.Y. *Herald-Tribune* for 20¢ an hour.

Travel Pages of Newspapers and Periodicals These are fast losing their credibility with me. Frequently, I cannot believe what I read! *The Globe & Mail* (Toronto) continues to publish articles on India which are untrue. Its editor is adamant and refuses to accept corrective information. It is my opinion that travel writers, in general, find it necessary to write only positive articles. (If they were to write the facts about Darjeeling in winter, such articles would not likely be accepted by the editor, who knows that advertisers and the travellers that the ads generate will not be attracted to the area.) On the other hand, no printed information was available when I needed it at the time of my photographic safari in

Passport and airline tickets are perennial tools of the trade.

Some people have funny logic

East Africa. I was interested in the predatory habits of a wide variety of animals in that region but could not find information on "who eats whom".

Holidays in Developing Countries   I must confess that I occasionally lose my patience when I see the list of holidays in some Third World countries – e.g., Nepal, with an Earnings per capita of $140 per year, follows a calendar with more than 45% non-work days! When the King travels to attend a funeral in another country, a holiday is declared on the day he leaves, as well as on the day he returns.

Ideology   Some people, when they become disenchanted with their government, take to the boats, as happened recently in Viet Nam, Cuba and Haiti, thereby presenting world federalist problems. We may curse some of their customs, but we should not allow innocent children to suffer. They are the common denominator – all God's children – and Ideology should not enter into it.

Now for the "nitty-gritty" of travel abroad:

International Conventions   A hotel can be a springboard which catapults you into a new world, or it can be a fortress which keeps you safe from being infected with strange ideas and emotions. . . .

This was demonstrated to me while staying, one time, at the big Inter-Continental Hotel in Colombo, Sri Lanka, in 1975. A four-day International Parliamentarians' Conference was being held there at the same time. (You notice that conventions are never held in Hoboken or Moose Jaw.) The day I saw that Canada was hosting a champagne luncheon, I stopped one of our MPs, as he was going into the luncheon, and asked when the delegates were going to take a tour of the island – to see at first hand some of its beauty and abysmal poverty. He looked puzzled and replied, "There isn't time for a tour. We've got too much of importance on the agenda." I thought it incredible that leaders from around the world were content to stay in that hotel, talking for four days, while losing the chance to learn something of this ancient land with all its joys and problems.

Accommodation Abroad   At least 60% of the time abroad I am privileged to be accommodated in private homes, which is arranged by the SCAW agency in that country. When, on several occasions, I was booked at a YWCA International Guest House, I took a lot of ribbing! The rest of the time, my budget restricts me to inexpensive hotels or other types of accommodation. Often I will choose a small pension or guest house, when possible. Not only are they more reasonably priced, but I get to meet people more readily.

Since the war, in Paris, many of the large old buildings have been converted into small hotels. This is particularly evident in the Champs Elysées area, where the lifts are often so confined that you have to turn your bag on end in order to ride up with it (I call these "after-thoughts" or "claustrophobia" elevators). And the rooms are not cheap in these small hotels!

South Africa and Singapore have provided me with some of the most comfortable accommodation and excellent service in my experience – probably a legacy from colonial times, when British administrators insisted on the best while travelling.

Japanese hotel designers cannot be beaten for all the conveniences they can cram into a wee area – even to a telephone in the bathroom (also a feature of Spanish hotels). And then there are the extra touches such as throw-away slippers and dressing gown.

In many European and Eastern hotels, one of the charming gestures which I've enjoyed is the custom of a flower, a wrapped chocolate, a piece of fruit, or sometimes even a local newspaper left on the bed in the evening when the maid turns down the sheets. It costs the hotel almost nothing but creates valuable goodwill. Our North American hotels could learn from this.

When prices quoted for rooms are sky high, I sometimes tell the front desk clerk that I don't want to *buy* the bed – I just want to *rent* it for a few hours – which usually elicits a pained smile. To get my money's worth out of a room at such a price, I would need to spend the entire 24 hours in the room.

Even if I were to agree to pay $60 a night for a room, there could be Extras. In some places, in the East, I've had to pay extra to have the room's air conditioner unlocked for my use. At the Sukontha Hotel in Haadjai, Thailand, I was quoted two prices – *with* or *without*. It turned out they meant with or without carpet.

As to rooms and service in Iron Curtain countries, it's always a seller's market. In practice, the purity of party doctrine gets sullied. They seem to work on the same philosophy as many western industrialist countries, where goods are priced not on cost or value, but on what the traffic will bear. I will sit up all night before I will let a situation dictate an exorbitant price.

Murray at the Modern Hotel at a stop-over in Roumania.

As to bedding, step off this continent and you constantly have to be content with marshmallow mattresses – murder on your back; more often than not, you can't even get a sheet of plywood to add firmness. In Stockholm, I checked into one of the hotels, flopped down on the bed, and realized that the mattress must be filled with straw. Yup, no mistake – it crunched with every movement! When I threatened to move out, they brought me up a stiff foam mattress and immediately took the other back (to the stable, I hope).

Then there are the pillows. We can send men to the moon, and we can send a temperamental assortment of hardware clanking around Mars, but Science hasn't been able to come up with a standardized hotel pillow, nor a constantly cool pillow, which would be a great aid to sleep in hot climates. In Seoul, the pillows were of the same size and rigidity as cordwood, and about as comfortable. It turns out they were packed with rice husks! Every morning, I woke up certain that rigor mortis had set in overnight, at least from the shoulders up. If I had enough room in my luggage, I would carry my own pillow.

Reading lamps pose a problem, too. Often they have only 40-watt bulbs cowering under thick shades. This makes reading, for more than five minutes, a prelude to blindness. In Amsterdam, it was a 25-watt bulb. When I was travelling for a living, I used to carry a 100-watt with me to use in Canadian hotels and motels, where 40-watt bulbs were quite common, too.

Keeping track of foreign currency and exchange rates can prove a challenge for the world traveller.

Eating Abroad   While most travellers tend to gain weight on a trip, I usually lose a minimum of ten pounds, for multiple reasons.

Rather than take chances on too many local eateries, once or twice a week I will head for the equivalent of our supermarket and spend an hour or more selecting items, for later consumption back at the hotel. Not only is this a learning experience (it tells a lot about what the native populace eats and what it costs), but along with a good book, it furnishes me with an excuse for a little party back in my room, devoid of meal taxes, service charges and even language hassles with restaurant personnel.

When I cannot do this, I seek out an international hotel, if there is one, and eat there. The Intercontinentals and Sheratons, Hyatt Singapore, Manila Hilton and the Ambassador in Bombay are all good. Another alternative is finding refuge in Chinese food, which I find agrees with me more than many highly spiced, exotic dishes.

Flies are the culprit, I am always thankful if fruit with skins – such as oranges, bananas, grapefruit, etc. – are in season. But boiled eggs – ugh! – I never want to look at eggs for months after returning home.

Most of my memorable meals have been breakfasts! I will never forget one I ate six years ago at The Meikle House in Salisbury, Rhodesia. Close behind are the breakfast buffets at Holiday Inns in Hong Kong, Manila, and Johannesburg. (It has been my experience that too many places just cannot put bacon and eggs, toast and coffee together in the proper order so as to have everything hot. . . . I call these zig-zag breakfasts.)

Even in Paris, dining is not what it used to be. Despite the devalued 1984 franc, meals are very expensive. The jammed-up table arrangements spoil any dinner enjoyment, as well. Worse still are the specialty luncheon places where you select your favourites, then stand to eat, and are jostled while eating. I call this "barbarism at the trough".

And Australians I find long on hospitality and generosity, but short on cuisine – the coffee served there, I would guess, is instant coffee 90% of the time. (Sorry Aussies. . .)

Health   I don't take any chances with my health. Before I leave, I take all the precautions, and then some. While I am travelling in tropical Third World countries, I never assume that ice cubes, for instance, are made with clean water, or that water bottles in hotels contain boiled water. I am also careful with local fruit. On fourteen trips around the world, I have had dysentery only twice. And each time I return from these countries, I visit Dr. J.S. Keystone in the Parasitology Clinic at the Toronto General for a series of tests.

Taxis   In the East, even a simple transaction like trying to find a taxi is fraught with delays and frustration. As ever, it's a feast or famine. When you come out of the airport, you either find a riot of taxidrivers who are prepared to fight each other for the privilege of overcharging you – or there isn't even a broken-down donkey available.

Inferior Service   Do not meekly accept rude behaviour, poor service, inedible food or lumpy beds. It takes time and effort to complain, but constructive beefing gets things changed. By the same token, be quick to give thanks, to express your appreciation of good service and of unexpected favours and cheerful attention.

Theft   In all my travels, I have never had anything stolen from a hotel room, which is a tribute to the general honesty of people and to good hotelkeeping. If a traveller does have something stolen from a hotel room, however, the important thing is to notify the hotel and local police, and to be certain to get the number of the police report, which will be needed when filing an insurance claim on arrival home.

Hotel or Duty-free Shops   I never, but never, purchase anything in hotel or duty-free shops. They are usually saddled with an exceedingly high rent, which they have to take out of the traveller. As to airport duty-free shops, their merchandise is over-priced, too, and they have a captive market in the traveller with the bit of foreign currency left to cash in.

Hotel charges   Another squeezeplay is by both the hotels and airlines. If you arrive in Cairo, for instance, at 4 a.m. one day and then leave again on a flight out at, let's say 10 p.m. the same day, you have to pay two nights' hotel charges (despite the fact you haven't even spent one night there). A *day rate* for a limited number of people checking in under such circumstances would mean a great deal, particularly when one has forty flights and has to stay in upwards of fifty hotels in a three-month period, as I do.

The Airlines   A new in-flight nuisance has come on the scene, in the form of an obnoxiously loud tape, which is played while cabin personnel demonstrate the handling of safety equipment. I question this practice.

Airports   What a fertile field for the Human Rights Commission! In Auckland, New Zealand, for example, the long runway leading to the Immigration desks is steeply *uphill*. My last experience there found me inching my baggage along for twenty minutes (under a mammoth wall-to-wall sign "Welcome to Auckland").

In Frankfurt, while waiting for a connecting flight to Bombay, I tried to find a drinking fountain, only to be told that there was no provision for water drinkers. (I guess the suggestion is that travellers should drink pop or beer, the pop being $1 US per tin, if one happened to have American currency.)

Over in Singapore, at their jazzy new terminal, they have oodles of dancing lights and waterfalls, but ne'er a luggage cart. I was told they would damage the tile floor!

On a connecting flight from Manila to Jakarta, I was forced to lug my bags the whole length of the huge terminal without even a moving treadway to give me a breather.

At the spanking new terminal in Manila, porters literally grabbed my bags from the taxi, piling them on with other passengers', then loading them on to the belt of the X-ray machine just inside the entrance door. Other porters hurriedly

Travellers sometimes have to work for their fun — here in western Australia, Murray's friends had to push the bus to get it started.

Duty-free shop

Murray's camera has been a constant travelling companion.

operated from the other side of the machine. A tangled mass of bags came out at the other end; these were then stacked again onto trolleys for dispersal. I lost sight of my carry-on case and, in a panic, raced up and down the departure check-in stations, just catching a glimpse of it as it was being lifted onto the belt, only to discover later that it was destined for another part of the world.

Manila airport is jungle organization at its worst. And entering Prague, the passenger has to go through a long, steep flight of stairs, creeping one step at a time to Immigration at the top level.

I have cited only a few of the many airports whose designers qualify for a leather medal!

Schiphol, Holland has the finest, cleanest and most efficient – and best designed – airport in the world, in my view.

Airport tax – is something I regard as skyway robbery, but if we're going to be skinned, at least it could be done efficiently. Why can't the airlines include the tax on your ticket, just like flight insurance, and refund it once every year or every three months to the airport concerned? This would be a paper transaction which would save hundreds of man-hours and barrel-loads of bad temper which erupts when travellers either forget about the tax or haven't any local money left.

And then there was the time in Lusaka airport when after calling every hotel for a bed and then having to bed down for the night on the Terminal floor. In the morning I was again assessed departure tax on my flight to Blantyre although I had never left the airport. Zapped in Zambia!

Aircraft design   As to seat comfort, the only wish I can make for aircraft designers is that, when they die, they be put into tight-fitting caskets!

The aisles are a problem, too. Narrow and cluttered, they barely afford access to the lavatory, let alone space for minimal movement or exercise. My long legs, which need stretching periodically, create a real problem, particularly on 6- to 10-hour flights. For a few years, I used to use the Exit jump seats for simple exercises – until an American Airlines senior attendant stopped me, saying that I might break the seats! When I seemed shocked at their fragility, she altered her reason . . . too many mothers used them for diaper changing. Now if everyone started exercising in the lavatories, the airlines would be faced with a problem of some magnitude! It's not a running or jogging track I'm advocating – just wider aisles or better aisle design.

Airline food   On the positive side, the food served, in flight, is consistently good, under the circumstances. In fact, I still remember an Air France luncheon served between Bangkok and Manila! I wish, however, that the airlines could find a way of providing a more convenient pipeline to fluids, which are so important when flying at 37 000 feet. Alcohol consumption, which should almost be a "no-no" in flight, as far as one's body systems are concerned, is usually the most readily available. The tea is often over-steeped and cold, while the coffee is instant (again). The food in airport restaurants is also notoriously over-priced and the service poor.

Luggage and Lockers   And then there are the inevitable luggage problems – particularly lost luggage. Can you picture the thousands of lost bags orbiting throughout Europe at this very moment? Apparently Warsaw Airport loses 15-20 bags a day! And then there are the luggage lockers, the best value being at Auckland, New Zealand, where you can store a large piece of baggage for up to 7 days for 50¢.

Border entry cards interest me. To the categories –
          Married __ No longer married __ Never married __
why not add *Happily married*?

* * *

East, West, Home Is Best   In my travels, I have often come across people who have visited a city or a country, fallen in love with it and plan to return home, resign, sell their property, and move. I tell these people that looking at a place through "vacation eyes" rather than "vocation eyes" can produce many surprises.

* * *

Margaret and I love Canada. It has been good to us and has something we cannot do without. As my plane hovers over the dancing city lights of Pearson International Airport in Toronto, a feeling comes over me which I find hard to describe – except that it's great to be home, back in Canada, *the finest country on earth —* our *Home Sweet Home!*

CHAPTER FOURTEEN

The Twelve

Life is real, life is earnest, and the grave is not its goal,
Dust thou art to dust returneth was not written of the soul.

TENNYSON

Margaret and I believe that Life has a purpose, and also that "Unto whom is much given, much is required."

SCAW provides an entry for introducing Christianity through practical application.

When we started with Sleeping Children Around The World, we had no clear idea of how we were going to raise money. I suppose that, instinctively, I felt that if we did our best, and if the project proved valid, we would get the money somehow.

Right from the beginning, I was reluctant to approach friends and business associates. I wanted to tap new sources of support, which we did.

Some people might accuse me of ignoring the problems at home – the people who need help here, which is a fair comment. There is so much need in the

Part of Margaret's team
working on donor labels

*Members of Margaret's team
preparing kit documents*

world that I suppose it doesn't really matter whom you help, as long as you help someone – but I know the difference between being poor in Canada and being poor in Bangladesh. For those not handicapped in any way, or old, I feel that to be poor in Canada is only a sort of way station, not the final destination, because there is hope in this country – hope that things will be different, if not for us, certainly for our children – even at this time of high unemployment and a depressed economy. It is when there is no hope for people, such as in the Third World, that we must work to improve conditions. The better reason, of course, is that *they, too, are God's children.*

When in Calcutta in 1983, Dr. Gordon Brown and I were told by Mother Teresa that people often faulted her for not doing more rehabilitation, using the quotation – "Give a man a fish and he will live for a day; teach him to fish and he will live a lifetime." Her answer, full of logic, was: "What if that man is too weak and impoverished to hold a rod and to pull in the fish?"

"Man cannot live by bread alone. . . ." We also recognize that . . . he cannot live without bread. More must be done by the "Haves" for the "Have Nots" of the Third World.

From our *1984 NEWSLETTER:*   "Another banner year for SCAW! We distributed 10 000 Slumber Kits in India, Pakistan, Jamaica, Philippines, Haiti and Indonesia. This was done in cooperation with the Salvation Army, Canadian Jesuits, Kiwanis and Rotary International.

"When our goal had been $1 Million and we met that, our next goal became 1 Million Slumber Kits. We are on our way, with your help!"

I believe in goals . . . but they must be goals not too easily attainable – goals one has to reach for. Our goal for 1985-86 is 12 000 beds.

SCAW has been at work in eighteen different Third World countries. From the first distribution of 200 beds the total has grown to 85 500 – imagine that many suffering children put to bed through the love and generosity of SCAW supporters! *Many of you will sleep better knowing you have put a child in its first bed.*

There is something mysterious and beautiful operating in this business of "giving" which sweeps in from Canada and other countries to the beyond. It seems that the more one gives, not only monetarily, the more one receives. It's almost as if the very act of giving trips a lever in a machine somewhere in the universe and the bells ring, the lights flash and the rewards just keep pouring out!

THE TWELVE?
Every time I talk to a group, or make a presentation, I talk about the need to have someone "waiting in the wings" – preferably someone younger than I who can roll with the punches. I find, now, that I can't always duck in time, as I did in the earlier years of SCAW.

Murray and Margaret and 1985 travellers: foreground *Mabel Wilmut;* front row *Nancy Martin, Margaret, Murray, Marjorie Quinney;* back row *Jim Sargeant, Bette Sargeant, June Brown, Gordon Brown, John Quinney*

Ideal would be a businessman or businesswoman who has had to struggle with his or her own business to make it a success – one who knows the sacrifices. A hard-headed approach to running an organization, one that has to be held together by one visit a year and by mail, is necessary. In addition, other criteria are: love of children, ability to withstand the physical, emotional and financial requirements of travel (the latter an average of $4500 a year) and a knowledge of photography. Stiff requisites, but we have been able to draw some truly splendid people during the past three years, and we hope to interest as many as twelve, perhaps.

Ken Ireland of Mississauga, Ontario accompanied me in 1983 on a distribution to the Caribbean. Recently retired, he has joined the SCAW squad.

Dr. Gordon Brown of Essex, Ontario, took his basic training with me in 1983 and in 1984 handled three countries for us. He took along a friend – Jim Dent – with him, and, believe me, their contribution took a big load off my shoulders.

Then John Quinney of Strathroy, Ontario, Past-President and Lieutenant-Governor of Kiwanis, accompanied by his wife, Marjorie, volunteered to take the trip with me. The Quinneys and I were privileged to be house guests of Divya and Jitendra Shah for a whole week while distributing kits in Bombay and area.

Marjorie was a great asset– so much so that I now think a three-member distribution team is ideal, with one member female. Any number above three could prejudice the operation – accommodation- and transportation-wise.

Thus far, we have been able to afford only one distribution per year, but we are hopeful that additional teams (four teams of three?) will make for an on-going distribution programme throughout the year.

Murray and Margaret in 1984

John Quinney wrote:

"This mission to S.E. Asia in February and March of 1984 for SCAW has been the highlight of our experiences. It is a tremendous project and undertaking. We truly thank you for the opportunity of being part of the programme."

Marjorie Quinney wrote, in part:

"We saw the joy of the children and their parents. We know the kits will be shared in the family.

"We saw the shacks and the squalor, but these people have a self worth, a dignity which they need to survive, and they are surviving."

Dr. Gordon Brown, in telling about distributing 1500 kits in five locations up in the Darjeeling and Kalimpong area with Jim Dent, wrote:

"Possibly the most interesting distribution took place in a dried-up riverbed down in a valley with a swinging suspension walk-over bridge across it. It was quite a sight to see the various families coming from all directions down the mountainside, and then later to see them leave with their new kits on their heads. Many of them had walked for five hours to get to the distribution point, and then had to walk back again the same day. Before their journey homeward they were given a ration of flat rice and powdered milk."

Jim Dent wrote that it was a great experience and that, while he had heard and read about the poor and needy children in the subcontinent of India:

"I was not prepared for what I saw. It was *Newsweek* and *National Geographic* coming to life, and it was not a pretty sight. . . . I could go on for hours. I wish there was some way that you people who make this all possible could somehow feel what Dr. Brown and I experienced as we represented you. Maybe I can best sum it up by quoting a portion of the 40th verse of the 25th chapter of Matthew: "Inasmuch as ye have done it unto one of the least of these my children, ye have done it unto me.""

Owing to Margaret's health, for the first time in 14 years I was unable to make the long annual trip in 1985. However, Gordon and June Brown took Jim and Bette Sergeant from Tillsonburg, Ontario, while Mabel Wilmut of Westmount, Quebec and Nancy Martin of Thunder Bay, Ontario accompanied John and Marjorie Quinney. Yes, these eight people came to our rescue, so that two distribution teams of four covered three countries each. It was an overwhelming gesture.

From my grandfather's Bible:
"And he ordained twelve, that they should be with him and that he might send them forth to preach."

Mark 3:14